Lucid Dreaming

How to Unlock Your Dreams

Zara L. Nooring

from various sources. Please consult a licensed professional before attempting any techniques outlined in this book.

By reading this document, the reader agrees that under no circumstances is the author responsible for any losses, direct or indirect, that are incurred as a result of the use of the information contained within this document, including, but not limited to, errors, omissions, or inaccuracies.

Table of Contents

Introduction

I sit on the ledge of the plane's floor and see the scenery below me becoming smaller and smaller. The landscape I know is but a speck in the distance as the plane goes higher. "Jump!" The instructor shouts at me. He gives me a slight push, and I fall forward out of the plane. I am in free fall, and my adrenaline is pumping! As the ground comes into focus, I realize the parachute won't open. Panic sets in as the landscape changes to reveal the ocean. I have no choice but to dive into the water.

I dive deeper and deeper underwater. My pulse throbs in my ears as I realize I don't have an oxygen tank on, and I am going to stop breathing soon. Out of the corner of my eye, I see another person waving at me. Is that a… No, it can't be! My mind is playing tricks on me because I need to breathe. The person is coming towards me, and I take another look. Yes! It is a mermaid! I realize I must be in a dream.

"I'm dreaming!" I say out loud, and suddenly my breathing becomes normal. Everything around me comes into greater focus. There is a community of mermaids and strange-looking underwater creatures. I get onto the back of a seahorse and ask it to show me around the waterscape. I think I have been here before, but for now, I simply enjoy the ride. I wonder what this dream has in store for me.

***

This anecdote reflects a lucid dream. It may seem crazy in real life, but it felt quite real while asleep. Take a moment and think about your strangest dream. What could you do in it and were you able to change some elements? Many people wake up after experiencing a lucid dream and wonder about what happened and whether it meant something. The dream felt so real that you might be questioning your very existence. I think Katherine Angela Yeboah explains this process best:

"You never know. Maybe when we're dreaming... we're more lucid than when we are awake."

Let's take one step back for a moment. A lucid dream occurs when you become aware that you are dreaming and gain some control over what is happening. It is an exhilarating experience that may come naturally to you or with some help from techniques. But, many lucid dreamers are left with questions when they wake up because they do not understand this phenomenon.

Lucid dreaming will make you ponder the very existence of life. You might wonder whether anybody can have a lucid dream, how you can have more lucid dreams, or if these dreams possess a spiritual component. Many people want to know if lucid dreaming is safe or whether it has bad omens. Some people fear getting stuck in dreams or worry about nightmares. I had these concerns too at one point, but it inspired me to learn more about lucid dreams and use my knowledge as a powerful tool for an improved experience.

My experience with lucid dreams started a long time ago. I have been lucid dreaming for as long as I can remember and find it fascinating. As an experienced lucid dreamer, I decided to pursue a career as a researcher in dream science for the past 10 years. I have extensive knowledge about lucid dreaming, inducing dreams, exercising control, and its amazing benefits. My knowledge comes from both self-experimentation and through studying the experiences of other lucid dreamers. I want to share this knowledge with you!

In this book, I will explore lucid dreaming with you and teach you everything you need to know. I will discuss the science and history behind lucid dreaming and its purpose in your life. You will learn techniques to improve your awareness while awake so that you can use these strategies when you are asleep. We will also explore different techniques to induce lucid dreams from the waking and sleeping state so that you have an arsenal of strategies to try out until you find the ones that work best for you.

Lucid dreams are exciting because the dreamer has some sense of control. I will show you methods to use this power so that you can create and change the narrative, landscape, events, and characters. Through a series of lucid dream challenges, you will get inspiration to do more in your lucid dreams and increase your understanding, creativity, and self-knowledge. These possibilities allow you to face your fears, boost your self-confidence, overcome nightmares, and affect you positively both in a mental and physical sense.

Lucid dreaming is a life-changing experience and has immense benefits. It allows you to immerse yourself into new worlds and events, understand yourself better, and boost your creativity. Lucid dreaming is a beautiful experience and allows you to escape from your waking reality. Through lucid dreaming, you become more aware of yourself and your surroundings in the waking and dream world. It encourages you to think deeply about your life, teaches you mindfulness strategies, and allows you to explore things you may not have access to in real life. With all these possibilities in mind, it only makes sense that you want to experience lucid dreams!

Anyone can experience lucid dreams, no matter your age, gender, religion, or ethnicity, so do not think for a moment that this book is not for you. In the past, you could have experienced lucid dreams and found them enjoyable and wonder about replicating this adventure. You may have heard that lucid dreams allow for sexual encounters and want to try this out firsthand, which you can do with induction techniques. Some people have wild imaginations and want to explore other places that are free from the physical constraints of the real world. If you are curious and ready for life-changing experiences, then read on for the best ride of your life!

Chapter 1:

The Dream World Can Be Lucid

Lucid dreaming occurs when you become aware that you are dreaming. It is a state of conscious observation even though you are asleep. With lucid dreaming, you are able to control some parts of your dream and the things happening in it. You might be able to control the characters, the environment, and the narrative. Basically, you can control everything in your dream—what an amazing ability!

What does it mean to become aware? Simply put, being aware is to take notice of everything. You pay attention to what you can see, feel, hear, smell, touch, and taste. Being aware requires conscious effort to notice how your body moves in time and space and even includes breathing.

All of these things may seem a bit foreign at the moment, so let's look at what other people have to say about lucid dreaming. These testimonials come from The Occult Blogger website.

"One of my most powerful lucid dreaming experiences was realizing I was dreaming. All of a sudden, I was in a large garden with millions of beautiful violet flowers. They were radiating, and I could smell the perfume from them. I remember it was a very clear day in the dream, where everything was glowing, and I felt so happy. I walked around and took in the wonder. A couple of times since then, I have found this same place when going into lucid dreaming. I always wake up very refreshed and helped for the day. I call it my violet healing experience." - Timon

"I have experiences with lucid dreaming all the time. When I am dreaming and think or say, 'I must be dreaming,' then I would look at my hand. When I am dreaming, my hand appears distorted. My fingers are odd sizes and shapes and usually have bruised fingernails, then I know I am dreaming and can control it. When I want to change my scenery or who I'm with, I try to spin. It feels like I am on a kid's ride at the park, holding onto the middle but pulling outwards until I stop. While I'm spinning, I concentrate on where I want to be and who I want to be with, and once I stop spinning, I am there." - April

Who Can Lucid Dream?

Lucid dreaming is an exhilarating experience, and the best part is that anyone can do it. Yes, that includes you!

Everybody dreams throughout the night. Some people remember their dreams while others forget what they dream by the time they wake up. Think about it this way; if you have ever remembered a dream after you wake up, then you are aware of your dreams to a limited extent. Lucid dreaming broadens this awareness and opens up a whole new world. Anybody who dreams, which is everybody, has the ability to become conscious while they dream.

Lucid dreaming can occur regardless of your age or cognitive abilities. Even children or individuals with life-limiting medical conditions can experience lucidity during the night. Anybody can lucid dream once they learn the right techniques and open themselves up to this experience.

Lucid dreaming requires awareness and habit. Recognizing that you are in a dream state is so important if you want to lucid dream. Some methods for recognition are rooted in habit, like meditation, visualization, reality checking, use of dream herbs, journaling, and use of mnemonic methods. There are also many ways to induce lucid dreaming—we will discuss all of these things in greater detail throughout this book.

The most difficult part is recognizing lucidity for the first time, but it becomes easier over time. Focusing on lucid dreaming takes patience, and you could experience lucidity within 3 to 21 days if you remain dedicated to the task. Just know that you can lucid dream and you will find a technique that works for you!

Van Eeden's Seven Types of Dreams

The Dutch psychiatrist and writer, Frederik Willem van Eeden, was a medical student in Amsterdam. Van Eeden, who lived during the late 19th century and the early 20th century, enjoyed a bohemian lifestyle and became one of the forefathers of dream literature. He spoke of mental clarity and proposed the term lucid dreaming after studying and experiencing various types of dreams.

Frederik van Eeden studied his own dreams and kept a journal of the most interesting ones. He documented approximately 500 dreams and more than 350 of them were lucid dreams! Van Eeden suggested that there are seven types of dreams.

Initial Dreams

The first type of dream identified by van Eeden is an initial dream, which is extremely rare. Initial dreams might occur if you fall asleep instantaneously when you are very tired but otherwise healthy. During this state, you feel and see just like in other dreams and could experience sensations like flying or floating. Van Eeden explains that you could become aware of being asleep, and specifically your fatigue, or that your body is experiencing physical strain. This type of dream could feel vigorous and refreshing.

Pathological Dreams

Generally, physical health does not have a great effect on a person's dreams. The exception, though, are pathological dreams, which occur when a person experiences indigestion, uses toxic substances, or has a fever. Many times, people experience these dreams as nightmares and have them shortly before waking up, although pathological dreams are quite scarce.

Ordinary Dreams

The most prevalent type of dream is called an ordinary dream and is experienced by everybody. Ordinary dreams have no clear direction, can be nice or awful, and even touch on being insane since they frequently contain elements of absurdity or confusion. Most people forget ordinary dreams by the time they wake up or only have a faint memory of what they dreamed.

Vivid Dreams

Vivid dreams can occur frequently, too, and make a strong impression on the dreamer because the dream is vivid. Dissociation usually happens with vivid dreams because they are quite absurd and have no link to reality. Vivid dreams may be linked to psychological distress but can occur when you are of sound mind too. Many people can remember vivid dreams for hours or even days after waking, which can be quite upsetting if the dream was unpleasant. Vivid dreams can be a positive experience, too, and even provide joy to a dreamer.

Demoniacal Dreams

Dreams that have mocking qualities or strange symbolism are called demoniacal dreams by Frederik van Eeden. These dreams occur from low moral thinking, although they are not necessarily "demonic" in nature. These dreams could include symbols that people store in memory or come from an unknown source. Demoniacal dreams could also include erotica or other obscene elements.

General Dream-Sensations

General dream-sensations describes a dream where a person constantly focuses on a person, object, place, event, or abstract thought. It is a state while sleeping where you are aware of something abstract, but the dream has no clear vision, story, names, or other specific elements. General dream-sensations refers to a sensation in dreaming and can be quite remarkable. Usually, they occur during deep sleep and can be recalled clearly after waking.

Lucid Dreams

The final type of dream is lucid dreaming, and van Eeden describes them as the most interesting of all dreams. With lucid dreams, a person has perfect awareness and can direct their attention with free will. The undisturbed sleep state while lucid dreaming leaves a person feeling refreshed and invigorated through creativity and problem-solving. Van Eeden believed that lucid dreams are worth careful observation because of their complexity and interesting characteristics.

Lucid dreaming may seem a bit strange and difficult to imagine if you have not experienced it before. But, you can get an idea of the lucid dreaming experience by comparing it to something with which you are more familiar—the conscious, awake state you are in now. It all centers on awareness.

Become Aware

One of the easiest ways to start becoming aware is to do a mindfulness exercise. Being mindful means you are living in the moment and that you are aware of what is happening at that exact point in time. The mental state a person gets into during mindfulness is similar to meditation, and you become aware, or lucid, within this moment. It is a great comparison to what you may experience during lucid dreaming. Try the following two-minute exercises for a similar experience to lucid dreaming.

Awareness in 5-4-3-2-1

Becoming aware of your senses forms part of meditation and uses mindfulness techniques to experience your current situation fully. This exercise is a fantastic option when you experience overwhelming emotion, such as during panic attacks, as it helps to focus your mind.

Keep your eyes open and follow these steps:

1. Use your sight to find five things you can see. Name the objects in your mind or out loud, and take a moment to observe each item fully before moving to the next object.
2. Identify four things that you can feel within your body. Name the sensation aloud or silently to yourself and take several deep breaths as you experience the sensation.
3. Listen for three sounds and name them silently or aloud. Pause to listen to each one while breathing deeply.
4. Identify two smells around you and name the smell aloud or in your mind. Breathe the smells in deeply.

5. Lastly, identify one taste, or if you cannot taste something, then think of a taste you like. Take a moment to reminisce on the taste.

For example, you could be sitting in the bedroom and experience the following things from this exercise.

- Five sight items: the garden outside, towels on the bed, the dog, a closet, and curtains.
- Four things I can feel: my chest rising up and down as I breathe, tingling in my fingertips, my dog's breath against my leg, and the cool air on my skin from the fan.
- Three sounds: a bird chirping outside, music playing, and the water fountain in the yard.
- Two smells: fresh coffee and cut grass.
- One taste: coffee on my breath.

Become Aware of the Breathing Process

This next exercise focuses on being aware of your breathing. Have you thought about your breathing yet? Most of the time, we don't realize we are breathing, even though it is something we do every moment of every day. Take notice of your breathing right now. Is it fast or slow? Are you taking deep breaths or shallow breaths?

Hold your breath for a few moments, then exhale slowly. Inhale deeply and feel how the air enters your body. Feel the air leave your body as you exhale. Focus on how your breathing changes as you concentrate on breathing. Become conscious of how you can manipulate your breathing and change it to your liking.

Become Aware of Your Emotions

Spend some time thinking about your feelings or emotions. Consider how you currently feel compared to how you felt this morning or yesterday. Just recall different emotions gently. Think about feelings like joy, anger, fear, sadness, excitement, and any other emotions you frequently experience.

Become Aware of Your Thoughts

What are you thinking at this exact moment? Take note of your thoughts while you are reading this book or during these lucidity-comparison exercises. Bring your current thoughts to the forefront of your consciousness and really feel them. Sometimes our thoughts seem real, while our thoughts may seem questionable at other times. Being aware of your thoughts is very important for mindfulness but also for lucid dreaming.

Become Aware of Yourself

You are doing these exercises, and you are reading this book, so are you aware of yourself? Your thoughts, emotions, and very being will always include you. Think about it as becoming aware of "I" or your ego. You hear, see, feel, think, breathe, and experience every emotion. You are the epicenter of your life and everything that happens in it.

Try the previous exercises again and focus on *your* feelings or personal role throughout each one. For example, in the 5-4-3-2-1 exercise, don't simply say, "the garden outside." Rather, say, "*I* see the garden outside." Focus on your presence and being in every moment.

Become Aware of Your Awareness

Can you feel yourself becoming more aware with each exercise? Most people with heightened awareness have a greater appreciation for their surroundings, moments, and what they are experiencing. Becoming aware of your awareness allows you to understand yourself and your mind better. It positions you relative to other things and your ego. Awareness enables mind training. You learn to switch on mental states by choice so that you can use your mind to its full potential.

Become aware of your own awareness with the following exercise. Visit a relatively busy location like a park or shopping center. Pay attention to specific objects or things, such as identifying people, smells, and where they are relative to other things. Use all your senses while observing the scenery around you. Let your attention move across the awareness spectrum and focus on different things. Concentrate on the bigger picture while focusing on your breathing. Become aware of yourself and your awareness.

Lucid Dreaming Versus Reality

How did you find these exercises that are similar to lucid dreaming? A lot of what you just experienced in the real world applies to the dream world too. The world of dreams is filled with rich multisensory experiences, which include seeing, hearing, feeling, thinking, and tasting. The main difference between the dream world and the real world is the origin of the experience. In the real world, you are exposed to external stimuli, while the dream world experience originates from an internal source.

All these experiences can be quite confusing, and many people question whether they are indeed awake or dreaming. The truth is that you will know in which mental state you are because your conscious mind helps you to understand reality versus the imagination. Usually, dreams limit your sensory experience because you are only aware of your immediate surroundings, while awareness, in reality, stretches further, such as hearing things in the street or beyond the area you find yourself in.

Many times you will know you are in a dream because the imagery and events are not realistic. For example, you might be at the beach but not remember how you got there, or maybe you don't even live close to the ocean. Another example is changes in the properties of your body—you might experience a distorted shape or be able to push your fingers through your body. A further example is to look around you in the dream and look for anything that cannot be real, such as strange creatures or landscapes. Your conscious mind while dreaming is filled with awareness, so you will realize you are in a state of dreaming and not reality.

The lines between dreaming and reality frequently blur when people experience false awakenings. A false awakening occurs when you wake up from a dream only to realize you are still asleep, or "trapped" in a dream state, and then wake to reality a few moments later. Many people find this experience distressing and worry that their dream is reality and they cannot escape. One of the most upsetting false awakenings occurs when you dream you have gotten up from bed, showered, and start going about your day, only to realize later that this situation is fake. Reality checking is absolutely necessary in this case because it will point out whether you are awake or actually dreaming by using your conscious awareness.

Benefits of Lucid Dreaming

By this stage, you should have a better idea of what lucid dreaming entails. I always get excited about lucid dreaming because it is such a wonderful experience! There are many reasons to lucid dream, and it can be beneficial. You can dream anything you want, even if it would seem unrealistic in the real world.

Relieves Emotional Distress

Lucid dreaming provides an escape from reality. It is a great break away from depression, anxiety, or general feelings of sadness. Many people who experience insomnia, which is difficulty falling or staying asleep at night, find that lucid dreaming gives them something to look forward to and helps them sleep more easily.

Reduce Nightmares and Overcome Fears

Everyone has something they are scared of, or maybe you struggle with nightmares. In some cases, nightmares about your fears can take over your sleep and leave you tossing and turning. It is absolutely awful, but lucid dreaming can be an escape mechanism and tool to cope. Lucid dreams are a safe space, so use them to deal with nightmares and overcome your fears. You can control your dreams—induce lucid dreaming to prevent nightmares. If you are having a lucid nightmare, then you can change the course of your dream.

Many people use lucid dreaming to face their fears. You control the dream world, so it allows you to induce your fear and deal with them in a safe manner or stop them at your choosing. For example, you might have arachnophobia, which is a fear of spiders, so you can imagine approaching a small spider or seeing different ones. Next, you might dream that you are holding a spider in your hand and work up to holding dangerous spiders. At any time, you can stop the dream and return to safety. As time progresses, you will find that you can handle seeing spiders in real life and not run from the room as soon as you see one. Lucid dreaming opens your world to more adventures and living a life without fear.

A New Perspective

Lucid dreams allow you to think about things that you may otherwise push to one side. Your mind and soul start talking to you while lucid dreaming, and many people find they are having conversations with their true self. They ponder questions about life, such as their true purpose at this moment and for the future. Suppressed thoughts may come to the surface while lucid dreaming and give you the opportunity to realize more about yourself. You learn more about yourself in a safe space free from the judgment of other people.

Dream Planning

You can have anything you want in your lucid dream, and the best part is that you can plan the plot before you even fall asleep. Want to travel to Atlantis in a submarine? Sure! What about rappelling the grand canyon or saving the world from a super-villain? You can do that too!

Think about the plot of your dream by using the wake-induced or dream-induced techniques, which you will learn about later, and you can create elaborate dreams to your heart's content. Being excited about a dream is likely to induce lucid dreaming, so build up as much anticipation as possible and think about the dream you want to experience frequently.

New Transport Methods and Dimensions

You don't need to walk, drive, or use other familiar transport methods in your lucid dreams. You can travel anyway you want! People frequently fly (by themselves) in lucid dreams or spin around and be where they want to be. You can travel to other countries, imaginary places, new time zones, or entirely different dimensions. Try to visit the past or future in your lucid dreams because you are working according to your chosen timeline and don't need to stick to any real-world characteristics.

Meet Other People

Think about someone you have always wanted to meet. It can be anyone; it doesn't matter if they are dead or alive. You can meet fictional characters, real people, superheroes, actors, activists, inventors, etc. The list is endless. You can concentrate on meeting new people and even plan out your conversations with them beforehand so that you can make the most of your dream time together. Just think about all the inspirational or academic conversations you might have!

Meeting new people in your dreams is quite spectacular, but you don't need to limit yourself. Many people experience sexual fantasies in their lucid dreams, which surprises them because they would never think of engaging sexually with someone else than their partner. This is one of the biggest reality checks for most individuals because they know they are dreaming. Sexual fantasies can make it easier to induce lucid dreaming, so it is a strategy to try if you are struggling to lucid dream.

Reunite With Others

Have you ever lost a person and wished you could speak to them one last time? I think most people have at least one person that they would love to hug and talk to because they were such a valuable part of their life. You can use lucid dreams to visit lost loved ones and communicate with them as if they were next to you.

Lucid dreaming is a type of therapy and can help you through the grieving process. It is a healing process to see a loved one in a lucid dream and being able to say some last words before letting them go. Lucid dreaming brings closure to many people, so induce memories of your loved one to see them a final time.

Increased Creativity

Obviously, lucid dreaming is full of creativity, and your imagination has no bounds. It only makes sense that your creativity will increase during this process. Lucid dreams are a creative outlet—your creativity will improve as you dream more and let your imagination run wild. Being creative also lets you solve problems while you dream, so your problem-solving skills improve too.

Improve Life Skills

You can improve your skills while lucid dreaming. Some people use their dreaming time to practice a specific skill or to prepare for an event coming up. For example, they might prepare mentally for a test or rehearse exercise moves. Some surgeons even mention practicing upcoming operations so that they are ready for every step. You might use your lucid dream to practice talking to people if you struggle with communication, or maybe you could prepare for an impressive presentation at work. The possibilities are endless, so use lucid dreaming to improve yourself and your skills.

Risks of Lucid Dreaming

Just as with anything, there are some risks to lucid dreaming. However, the benefits far outweigh the risks of lucid dreaming since there are only two real risks. That is awesome news because you can lucid dream without worrying about it being dangerous, especially if you are aware of the risks.

Decreased Sleep Quality

Lucid dreams are vivid, which can wake you up. You might also be focusing more on lucid dreaming than actually sleeping, and that can decrease your quality of sleep. Some methods you will learn to induce lucid dreaming can cause you to get less sleep or decrease your quality of sleep. Sometimes, people wake from lucid dreams and struggle to get back to sleep, which also means they are getting less sleep, and they could feel tired the next day. It might be a good idea to stay away from lucid dreaming in the days preceding a big event that requires energy and focus.

Confusion or Delirium

Lucid dreaming can cause confusion in some people. Individuals with mental health problems are at risk of experiencing delirium or hallucinations when they lucid dream, especially if they cannot distinguish between reality and imagination. Lucid dreams can occur naturally, though. This situation is difficult to control, so be aware of this risk if you or a loved one has mental health disorders.

History of Lucid Dreaming

If people have been around for centuries, then it only makes sense that lucid dreaming has existed for the same amount of time. History is full of lucid dreaming since important people cataloged their dreams while others studied dream science to get a better understanding of their experiences. Regardless of time, background, or religion, all people share dreaming throughout history.

Hinduism and Buddhism

Lucid dreaming was documented in the *Upanishads* before 1000 BCE. It was found in Hindu proverbs, philosophy, and spiritual lessons. Another text, called the *Vigyan Bhairav Tantra*, explains how to alter consciousness so that you can change dreams and reach different sleeping states. The Bonpo have used meditation and lucid dreaming together for more than 12,000 years after Indian influence reached various areas of Tibet.

The Tibetan Book of the Dead documents the merger between shamanic culture and Buddhism. This book was translated partially by Walter E. Evans-Wents during 1935. This partial translation made Western occultists and historians realize that lucid dreaming dates back to ancient times across the world and cultures. It also gave insight into different practices that dream scholars could use during the 20th century and throughout psychological teachings.

Classic Greece

Classic Greek literature discusses dreams at length. Influential Greek philosophers such as Aristotle, Plato, and Socrates all spoke of reality versus dreams and mentioned the presence of consciousness while dreaming. One of the earliest documented dream texts is called *On Dreams*, which was written by Aristotle in about 350BC. By 415AD, St. Augustine wrote a report on a lucid dream a patient experienced, even though the exact term had not yet been found for this type of dream.

Islam

The history of Islam contains accounts of lucid dreams and played a crucial role in the tenets of the religion. Spiritual initiation first occurred during a nighttime vision by Mohammed, which he reported in the *Lailat al-Miraj*. Later on, Sufi Ib al-Arabi explained that controlling dreams is an important mystic ability. Shamsoddin Lahiji, another Sufi mystic, also spoke of a nighttime vision that appears to be a lucid dream, three hundred years after recognition by other Islamic figures. There are many differences between historical and cultural accounts, so there is no certainty about these accounts, but these events were through periods of lucidity, regardless of whether the person was awake or asleep.

A Dark Time for Lucid Dreams

Lucid dreams had a good classical beginning but Judeo-Christian culture dampened the study of lucid dreams in Imperial Rome. Theologians during this time believed that dreams connected to a greater truth but also believed that some spread lies. Thomas Aquinas furthered this idea during the Middle Ages and took it a step further by saying that lucid dreams could be from demons, so Christians in the West refrained from expressing lucid experiences. Many Western cultures still push the idea of dreams to one side due to these superstitions.

The Enlightenment Period

European cultures embraced reasoning during the 17th century and made space for lucid dreaming. Dreamers and philosophers like Thomas Reid and Pierre Gassendi started talking about their dreams. *The Olympica*, a personal journal written by René Descartes, documents his experiences of lucid dreaming, but he kept it secret due to his role in the scientific community and in the church.

The next big break for lucid dreaming came from Frederik van Eeden in his text, *A Study of Dreams*, that mentions the seven dreams we looked at earlier in this chapter. Van Eeden also came up with the term "lucid dreaming" to describe the experience. Later on, during the 1960s, Celia Green made connections between certain dreams and REM sleep, and psychologist Keith Hearne finally provided scientific evidence of lucid dreaming in 1975. However, this research was not found in popular scientific journals until 1978, when Stephan LaBerge became the leading force of lucid dreaming after publishing data about the experience. This research brought more life to lucid dreaming literature.

Lucid Dreaming and Spirituality

The connections between lucid dreaming and spirituality have been around for centuries and could be part of the reason why theologians suppressed the concept. But, spirituality does not equate to religion, even if there are similar concepts. Let's look a little more at lucid dreaming and how it can be a spiritual experience for you.

Being spiritual and lucid dreaming both require greater levels of awareness. In "normal" dreams, you are unaware of your emotions, physical state, and other things going on around you. This all changes when you have a lucid dream because you are more aware of everything, no matter its size, position, or importance.

Lucid dreaming enhances awareness while you sleep, but the techniques to induce lucid dreaming are similar to meditation and relaxation techniques used while you are awake. So, you could argue that being more aware during lucid dreams allows you to be more aware in daily life. Spirituality requires that you be aware of everything in life and your position relative to everything else. Being aware and conscious of things while awake allows you to become more present and calmer; it provides perspective in everything you set your mind to.

Lucid Dreaming vs. Astral Projections and Reality Shifting

There is quite a bit of confusion between lucid dreaming, astral projections, and reality shifting. These concepts do not mean the same things and have specific characteristics. It helps to understand these differences so that you can practice lucid dreaming properly. Keep in mind that lucid dreaming occurs when you have increased awareness while dreaming. You can alter your dream and environment, and you can stop the dream at any time—you are in control during the entire lucid dream, and it is not real.

Astral projection occurs with full consciousness and before you fall asleep. It is a very real experience where a person travels along the astral plane to a dimension that is external to the real world. The place a person travels to, narrative, and other elements cannot be controlled by the person, although you might be able to manipulate some interactions and conversations. The experience ends when consciousness returns to a person's physical body. Astral projections can be quite dangerous unless you have been properly trained in this art, so do not try this without extensive preparations.

Reality shifting is another topic that is sometimes confused with lucid dreaming, but they are entirely different. Reality shifting occurs when you make a conscious decision to move from one reality to another.

For example, your current reality is reading this book while other realities such as soccer games are going on elsewhere. You choose the reality you want and have the power to make conscious shifts.

Lucid dreaming has a fascinating history and is as much a part of historic figures' lives as it is a part of society today. Lucidity has gone through many adaptations and interpretations, and it remains a powerful element of dream literature. Today, lucid dreaming is welcomed more easily, and many people have started speaking about their experiences. The benefits of lucid dreaming far outweigh the concerns, so open your mind to the possibilities, and you will find a new world revealing itself to you.

Chapter 2:

How Do You Dream What You Dream?

Often, we wonder how dreams happen and why we dream certain things. There is quite a bit of science behind dreaming; therefore, many things contribute to dreaming. Dreams can be interesting or boring, bizarre or realistic. Sometimes, your dreams feel real or are filled with recent events that you have been thinking about. Dreams can be all-consuming, so understanding the science behind dreaming can help to understand some of what happens.

Sleep and Dream Cycles

What are dreams? This question is a tough one that many people wonder about. Some people refer to dreams as the wishes of your mind, while others believe that dreams are your thoughts while sleeping. Dreams are a part of memory and might be realistic or fake. Sleeping helps you process memories, and this may be part of the reason why your dreams are filled with recent events. A vivid imagination could be part of unrealistic dreams, such as those experienced during lucid dreaming.

Dreams are a result of the stage of sleep you are in. In the previous chapter, seven types of dreams were discussed, and these dreams depend on the type of sleep you are experiencing. Sleep is characterized into two categories: REM (rapid eye movement) and NREM (non-rapid eye movement). Dreams during NREM sleep are quite ordinary and may contain memories, while REM sleep frequently results in jumbled memories or lucid dreaming.

NREM sleep has three stages, while REM sleep only has one stage. With all three NREM stages, a person has little muscle activity and low eye activity, and their dreams are short. NREM stage one occurs just after falling asleep and early on in the night. Stage two NREM occurs throughout the night, while stage three usually happens earlier during sleeping. In contrast, REM sleep has no muscle activity as a person almost enters a state of paralysis, while eye movement increases rapidly and repeats several times during the night. REM sleep allows dream recall and creativity, which relates to lucid dreaming.

The Science of Lucid Dreaming

There is a lot of science that backs up lucid dreaming. Researchers and philosophers from previous centuries paved the way for further research into lucid dreaming. Although Keith Hearne and Stephen LaBerge had major breakthroughs in lucid dreaming research, scientists and other professionals want to understand lucid dreaming better. People want to understand the induction, neurology, and physiology of lucid dreams, as well as their unique benefits.

REM Sleep

Celia Green had a prolific finding when she found a link between dreaming and REM sleep. A person enters a deep sleep characterized by quick eye motions (thus the name REM), increased brain activity, and faster breathing. Most people experience REM sleep for approximately 10 minutes when they have been asleep for 90 minutes. The REM process continues as you sleep, and each REM cycle is longer than the previous one until REM reaches a duration of about an hour.

This research was furthered by Hearne and LaBerge during the 1970s. Both found that REM occurs while people dream, and eye movement could even "signal" awareness or consciousness during dreams. Hearne proved this by recording eight left-to-right eye movements of dream participants by using REM polygraph paper. One of his specific participants was Alan Worsley who frequently had lucid dreams and used eye movement to communicate during dreaming. This process is called "eye signal verification" and has been used in subsequent research studies.

Eye signal verification is popular in recent research studies on lucid dreaming. For example, once participants are aware that they are in the dream state, they move their eyes four times from left to right, followed by moving their eyes twice after the start of the experiment, and then giving a signal again at the end of the experiment before waking up. The fact that participants can communicate while being asleep already indicates that they are conscious and aware to some degree.

Later Scientific Research in SLEEP

SLEEP is a scientific journal that featured several articles on lucid dreaming. A 2009 study on lucid dreaming recorded brain activity through a 19-channel electroencephalogram (EEG). The researchers, including Allan Hobson and Ursula Voss, found waking activity in the front parts of the cerebral cortex while a person is in REM sleep. This combination of REM sleep and waking activity is defined as measurable hybrid consciousness.

A 2012 research study focused on brain activity during lucid dreaming and compared it to other dreaming states during REM sleep. The researchers measured brain activity by using EEG and functional magnetic resonance imaging (fMRI) tests so that they could gather as much information as possible. The data indicated that more parts of the brain were active during lucid dreaming than with other types of dreams. These parts of the brain typically relate to awareness and self-reflection, which are major components of lucid dreams and factors that many lucid dreamers mention in discussions about their dreams.

Dreams and Science

Sometimes, a dream is ridiculous, like when your mother turns into a bird. Other times, dreams are so realistic that you startle as you wake, such as when you are dreaming about being in a car accident. Even if your dream is unrealistic, you may still experience a heart-pounding shock and feel as if something awful or amazing just happened to you.

Dreams can feel real, and science backs up this idea. During the 1700s, scientists believed that dreams occur because a person's imagination is the only section of the brain that functions as you sleep. The area of the brain that verifies reality does not always function during sleep, and that means a person believes everything they dream. Keep in mind, though, that lucid dreamers know they are dreaming, so this science has changed over the years. A person that is unaware of dreaming may experience their dreams as real.

Sigmund Freud, a 20th-century neurologist, believed that dreaming is a method to fulfill dreams. A classic example of wish fulfillment is wet dreams, where a person experiences sexual events as real. Freud mentions that dreaming can provide healing or be emotional but only if a person believes that a dream is real. To believe dreams, Freud says that a person's subconscious will repress critical thinking and doubt about things being fake. Even if a person's dreams are unrealistic, they may include dream symbols, which helps a person understand a situation. That is why Freud indicates that dreams have a healing role.

These days, scientists continue to study dreams. They have new technologies such as EEGs, magnetic resonance imaging (MRI), and computerized tomography (CT) scans to help them detect brain activity during sleep and dreams. Scientists and researchers also talk to study participants about their dreams to measure recall and perceptions. Many researchers agree with Freud as studies found that the part of the brain responsible for rational thinking deactivates while a person dreams and makes dreams feel extremely real. All of these things allow us to understand dreaming and its effects better.

Expectations and Perceptions

Expectations are beliefs we hold about something before we experience it. Expectations can be based on previous experiences or on something a person reads or hears from someone else. For example, you might expect to dream at night because you usually dream at night, or, if we make it very practical, you expect to find a specific type of milk at the grocery store because that is where you usually purchase this milk.

Expectations set the scene for how a person will experience a situation. These experiences result in a conscious understanding of events, which is called perception. Perception is influenced by external stimuli and internal processing, such as seeing, feeling, and hearing. Once a person experiences an event, they take in all kinds of information and process it through cognitive function, including expectations, to affect a person's beliefs of the situation.

Perception includes two processes. The first process is sensory input—this could be going to the store and standing in front of the milk aisle to observe all the different types. The second process requires cognitive processing of the sensory input, so you might realize that the brand of milk you want is on the bottom right shelf. Your perception of this experience is positive because the external stimulus agrees with your previous experiences and expectations. In contrast, you might have a negative perception of a store if they no longer stock the specific milk you want because it does not agree with your expectations.

The milk example is very basic, but the same process happens many times during the day and includes dreaming. Expectations and perceptions are part of our brain function as neurons (brain cells) communicate and store information. Our perception is powerful because it usually relates to expectations—if you expect to dream, then dreaming at night creates positive perceptions. Dreaming is also a brain function so you can control it through expectations and perceptions, and this is especially important in lucid dreaming.

Schemas as Building Blocks

Our perceptions, expectations, and thoughts are built on specific bits of knowledge. A schema is a concept that allows a person to organize, process, and understand information. Schemas establish specific ideas so that we can recognize them throughout life and react accordingly. They are the building blocks of our minds, just like bricks are the building blocks for a large establishment.

Types of Schemas

There are various schemas that develop throughout childhood and the rest of your life. Schemas can be placed into categories that each have their own characteristics, and your schemas depend on your upbringing, learnings, and specific situation. There are some schemas that are familiar to all people. Focusing on those can help you understand some of the schemas in life.

Person schemas relate to specific individuals and may include appearance, personality, and behavior. For example, your best friend may be short, have long brown hair and green eyes (appearance), love animals more than people (personality), and be introverted with good manners (behavior). These characteristics help you identify your best friend. In contrast, not recognizing someone alerts you to them being a stranger. You might associate a person that smiles with being friendly because a person you know always smiles and has a likable personality. Similarly, you might think a person who frowns is in a disagreeable mood, even if you do not know them in person.

Self schemas are beliefs and knowledge you have about yourself. It includes all the elements of your personality, ideals about the future, and how you perceive yourself. For example, you may be an extrovert who loves being around people and enjoys playing sports but dislikes board games. All these characteristics are schemas, and other people use these indicators to understand you.

Object schemas refer to a person's ideas about inanimate objects. Think about transport methods for a moment. As a child, you might think anything with wheels is a form of transport and could be calling everything with wheels a car. Later on, you learn that there are motorcycles, trucks, cars, bicycles, and so on. Other object schemas include food items, furniture, buildings, toys, and sports equipment.

Social schemas determine how a person behaves in certain social settings. Greeting a person when you see them, respecting your elders, and dishing up a reasonable amount of food are all behaviors exhibited in social settings. A similar type of schema is an event schema, which dictates behavior and beliefs. For example, you shake a person's hand when going for an interview or remain quiet while in a religious place.

Schemas rely greatly on a person's perceptions and expectations. Once you learn something specific, you regularly associate this information with other situations. Schemas become the building blocks for everything you know, how you act and react, and recognizing things in different situations. Schemas allow a person to make assumptions so that they can understand things when they only have partial information.

Building and Changing Schemas

Schemas start as soon as a child is born and increase rapidly as a child grows up. Children quickly learn new things and process information to build more schemas. Thinking back to the example of transport methods, we saw that there are many types of vehicles. Within the schema of cars, a child later builds schemas about a sports car, sedan, coupe, and hatchback, which further broadens their information set. As adults, learning continues, but schemas rarely change greatly because adults have specific perceptions.

Schemas change through assimilation and accommodation of information, specifically when information is known. Assimilation occurs when new information is added to preexisting schemas, such as when a person learns there is a new model of their favorite car. Accommodation occurs when a person changes a schema or forms a new schema in response to new information or experiences. For example, you might require a lot of evidence that women in the workplace have a valuable contribution if you grew up in a patriarchal society.

Three Parts of the Mind

Schemas form part of the brain as they are encapsulated by neurons, which organize thoughts and processes. Freud asserts that the mind consists of three parts, specifically, the unconscious, preconscious, and conscious mind. A schema that lies dormant is part of the unconscious mind, while a schema in the preconscious mind might activate other schemas but not enter consciousness itself. Once a schema activates, which is to take form, it becomes part of your conscious experience.

For example, the word "waterfall" was part of the unconscious mind until you read it. Now that it has been activated, it activates other schemas into consciousness. You might think about water cascading down mountains, a spray of water on your skin, and fishing in the river. Other schemas relating to "waterfall" may be in your preconsciousness because they don't have as great an association. You might have hiking or camping in your preconsciousness but only think about these things if you consciously think about where you stay when visiting a waterfall.

A Schema Example

Let's look at a tangible example of schemas and the role they play in our lives. Think about the story of Little Red Riding Hood. She went to visit her grandmother in the woods and found her lying in bed. Little Red Riding Hood asked her grandmother, "Why are your ears so big?" and her grandmother answered, "So I can hear you better."

What do you know about the brief story snippet (just the snippet, not the entire story) above?

- Little Red Riding Hood is visiting her grandmother.
- The grandmother is in bed.
- Little Red Riding Hood realized her grandmother's ears are different and asked about them.
- The grandmother responded.

Now, think about things you can infer about this story:

- Little Red Riding Hood is naive and possibly a child.
- Her grandmother looks strange.
- Her grandmother is old and sick (because she is in bed).
- The grandmother lives far away.
- The girl can see (she isn't blind).
- Her grandmother is lying.
- The grandmother is a wolf.

As you can see, a person makes many assumptions about a situation even if it is not fact. Nowhere in the snippet does it describe a wolf, that the grandmother is sick and lying, or that she lives far away. These are all things a person assumes because they already know the whole story. So, schemas help us understand things based on previous experiences and expectations, but how does this relate to dreaming?

Perception and Dreams

The process of perception changes when a person sleeps. During REM sleep, a person's brain is highly active, but they do not experience external stimuli, which is the first part of perception. Instead, brain activity enhances schemas higher than their perceptual threshold, and the schemas become part of your consciousness. You start to have sensory experiences while dreaming that would not be present as external stimuli if you were awake. Changing your perception during dreams is very challenging, so schemas play a huge role in your brain activity.

Dreams frequently include fragments of real-life perceptions. Schemas activated above the consciousness threshold become the events a person is most likely to dream about, especially if you expect to dream about something. Lucid dreamers construct their dream worlds while they are still awake so they are activating specific schemas. Many times, dream worlds are based on previous dreams or experiences so these perceived worlds become expected as you dream. The real world we experience includes time, space, air, and gravity, so the dream world usually includes these elements in some form too.

Why Dreams Are Meaningful

Neuroscientists do not agree on whether dreams have meaning or not. There is a lot of conflict in the data, but neuroscientists remain interested in the meaning of dreams and their role in a person's daily life. Ancient Egyptians believed that dreams are a blessing and give insight into the future, while Carl Jung and Sigmund Freud believed that dreams display characteristics of a person's mind. In contrast, Robert McCarley and J. Allan Hobson believed that dreams are meaningless and result from random triggers.

Whether you believe dreams have meaning or not doesn't matter. What is important is that the interpretation of dreams reveals information about our personalities and innermost workings. Dream imagery comes from people's minds and may or may not have messages. However, your dreams are personal and reveal deep truths about yourselves. They can motivate you, highlight discrepancies in your life, or just be a source of entertainment. Dreams are meaningful.

Linking Back to Lucid Dreaming

Assumptions are dangerous, and yet people's lives are full of assumptions. We already spoke about schemas and changing them through assimilation and accommodation. These schemas guide thoughts and understanding while awake but also rule during sleep and dreams. A person assumes their experience is real whether they are awake or dreaming and distorts their reality to fit with their assumptions. People constantly assimilate and accommodate dreaming so that their dreams can be possible. Once a person realizes something is unusual, they start to rationalize events and reduce assumptions.

Lucid dreamers must overcome their assumptions and schemas if they want to have fulfilling dreams. They have to accept that the reason for some unusual events is that they are dreaming and stop assimilation. Once you practice the accommodation of schemas, your dream can take any shape you want because your assumptions are not set in stone as you are aware of the dream state. Keep an open mind when it comes to dreaming, especially lucid dreaming, and let go of your assumptions if you want to have the full experience.

Chapter 3:

Preparation Is Key

Lucid dreaming might come naturally to you, or you can learn how to do it. Even if you lucid dream without giving much thought to it, you might want to improve your dream experience. Preparing for lucid dreaming is one of the most important things you can do. It will help you recognize the dream state, enhance your awareness, and improve your abilities within the dream.

Characteristics of Lucid Dreams

The literature on lucid dreaming constantly evolves, and more characteristics are coming to the forefront. Understanding the characteristics of lucid dreaming will help you prepare for the actual dreaming process. It also increases awareness and helps you move to a greater state of lucidity.

Lucid Dream Features

Paul Tholey was a German psychologist who suggested that lucid dreams have three features that differentiate them from ordinary dreams. Firstly, a person is aware of their consciousness and knows they are dreaming. Secondly, the dreamer understands they can manipulate events and make their own decisions while in the dream. Finally, consciousness is heightened to such a level that a person might be even more aware than had they been awake.

Levels of Lucid Dreaming

Lucid dreaming can vary in intensity depending on how lucid a person is during the dream state. Your lucidity in any dream depends on your perception of events, how much you control what is happening, the length of a dream, and clarity of mind. As you become more aware of your dreaming and become more lucid, you will experience these factors more intensely.

a. Non-Lucid Dreams

At its most basic, dreams are non-lucid, and this is a level that many people experience. It is a default state where a person is unaware of their dreams and accepts what they are dreaming as reality. Non-lucid dreams are irrational and vague or detailed and energetic. The dreamer is not aware of their dream and cannot control any elements since the entire dream stems from a person's unconscious mind.

b. Level 1: Semi-Lucid Dreams

Semi-lucid dreams are the lowest level and frequently experienced by beginner lucid dreamers. Most likely, the Dream Induced Lucid Dreaming technique (which you'll learn about in Chapter 4) was used to reach this state, and you are conscious of dreaming. Controlling events during semi-lucid dreams is difficult because your awareness is not that great and reality checking or stabilization is absent. Sometimes, people forget they are in a dream and lose their lucidity. Improving your conscious awareness will help you to get over this hurdle and establish rules for lucid dreaming that do not interrupt your dream.

c. Level 2: Fully Lucid Dream

With practice and determination, you could experience fully lucid dreams. Controlling events does not happen immediately with fully lucid dreams, and you need to work on different elements one at a time. The first thing to control is remaining aware within the lucid dream for longer periods of time. Next, you might control the environment, objects, conversations, and other elements.

An intense, fully lucid dream occurs when you are entirely aware of dreaming. You do not doubt your whereabouts and consciously choose to continue dreaming. The dreams are intricate, and you place no limits on your imagination. You can move around as you want or be a passive observer of the things happening in your dream.

d. Level 3: Dream Dissolving

You might think that a fully lucid dream is the highest level a person can reach, but you can surpass this level of lucidity to reach dream dissolving. Becoming so lucid that you surpass the dream state is possible and relies heavily on being aware of your awareness. With dream dissolving, a person goes beyond sensory experiences such as images, sounds, and tastes and moves into a stage where they simply experience heightened conscious awareness.

Signs You Can Become a Lucid Dreamer

Many people wonder whether they have lucid dreams or can experience lucid dreaming. You are probably one of these individuals since you are reading this book. Lucid dreaming has piqued your interest, and you might be wondering whether you are a natural lucid dreamer. Even if you haven't experienced lucid dreaming, you could still have an innate ability to lucid dream or learn the techniques. Here are some of the signs that you could be a lucid dreamer.

You Wake Up Naturally

A blaring alarm clock interrupts your sleep and forces you to wake up, which means you have less time to dream. If you wake up naturally, without the sound of an alarm clock, then you are going through the different stages of sleep by yourself and getting complete sleep cycles. REM sleep gets longer as you progress through the night, so many people experience lucid dreams shortly before they wake up.

Intense Dreams

Individuals who experience intense dreaming usually have the ability to lucid dream. Your dreams may be intense because they are vivid due to REM sleep or because you have some level of dream awareness. Dreaming is a motivational tool, and you often find inspiration in dreams, so they have a lot of meaning to you.

Remembering Your Dreams

Lucid dreaming occurs easily if you can recall your dreams because it shows a sense of awareness. Remembering your dreams allows you to think about the dream world and build upon it during the daytime. Thinking about the dream world enables you to return to it at a later stage and gives you greater control of your dreams.

Waking Yourself From Nightmares

Nightmares can manifest as lucid dreams and be very scary. Sometimes, a person can wake themselves from their nightmare by shouting "wake up" or realizing that what is happening is not real. If you can do this, then it means you were lucid and can lucid dream in the future. Some people use lucid dreaming to explore their nightmares and try to find out more about their fears because it is a safe space.

Controlling Your Dreams

Many people want to control their dreams just like they control their day-to-day life. Dreams manifest in your thoughts, beliefs, and emotions; therefore, you can have lucid dreams if you decide to have them. Think about lucid dreaming and state that you want to have a lucid dream during the day to boost control of your sleep and dreams.

Previous Lucid Dreams

Any person who has had a lucid dream before can have lucid dreams again. You might not have realized it was a lucid dream at that precise moment, but you know that you were aware of dreaming or could change some things. You should use this experience as a motivation for future lucid dreaming endeavors, and always remember that you can do it even if you are struggling to lucid dream.

Sleep Paralysis and Out-Of-Body Experiences

Many lucid dreams start with out-of-body experiences or sleep paralysis. Muscle activity is low during REM sleep, so you might feel paralyzed in your sleep and while lucid dreaming. Out-of-body experiences are quite common too. If you have ever experienced floating outside of your body, then you could easily lucid dream.

Discussing Your Dreams

Some people enjoy discussing their dreams with others or make notes about their dreams in a journal. These practices indicate that dreams intrigue you, and you want to know more about them. Writing down your dreams or talking about them also gives you a chance to explore your dream world more and increases your chances of lucid dreaming.

Intense Daydreaming

Individuals who daydream are quite likely to have lucid dreams. You might build new worlds and evocative stories while daydreaming. These visualization techniques can help you to induce lucid dreams and give you an advantage because your imagination is wild.

Routine Meditation

Some people are in the habit of meditating several times per week. Meditation increases your awareness and helps you to stay in the moment, which is essential during lucid dreaming. In essence, a person who meditates has the power to practice awareness while they are asleep.

Playing First-Person Video Games

First-person video games feature simulated realities where you control the narrative to some extent. They also provide you with spatial awareness, which is necessary for lucid dreaming. If you can control your game persona and reality, then you can also affect your awareness in lucid dreams.

Preparing for Lucid Dreams

Lucid dream preparation is not difficult at all. It consists of a few steps that you can include in your daily life easily. First, you need to start a dream journal so that you can learn more about your dreams. Secondly, you have to improve your ability to recall dreams so that you can write them down and identify different things about them. Thirdly, catalog your dream signs so that you are aware of them while dreaming. Next, you need to set goals for lucid dreaming and make time for lucid dreams. Finally, practice attentive relaxation so that you are ready to learn lucid dreaming induction techniques. Before we look at each of these steps, I want to address some concerns you might have about lucid dreaming, as these could be obstacles in preparing for lucid dreams.

Concerns About Lucid Dreaming

One of the biggest worries is that lucid dreaming leads to poor sleep or tires out a person. The risk of having poor sleep due to lucid dreams is very small because it happens in a normal sleep state (REM). The main reason that your sleep quality may decrease is that you are spending a lot of time inducing lucid dreams. Some people do find constant lucid dreams emotionally draining, so you might choose to switch off your lucid abilities once you do a reality check.

Another worry is getting stuck in a dream, but this cannot happen because it is just a dream. Saying "wake up" in your dream frequently jolts you from a lucid dream or lets you change the direction of your dream. All REM sleep cycles stop at some time, so even if you feel stuck or cannot escape a dream, it will come to an end naturally once REM sleep ends. A similar concern is that a person will die in real life if they die in a lucid dream, which is false too. It is a dream and you will be alive when you wake up.

You do not need to worry about being less alert during the day either. Lucid dreaming encourages awareness since you are practicing techniques that will improve your waking hours too. Lucid dreaming allows you to learn more about yourself, so do not hide behind your lucid dreaming fears.

Dream Journaling

A dream journal is a place to capture all your dreams and helps identify signs, techniques, and other relevant elements. Most people write down their dreams after waking up because that is the moment when the dream is freshest in their minds. Follow these steps when writing in your dream journal:

1. Get a notebook dedicated to only dream journaling, and keep it close to your bed. It should be near enough that you can reach it

without getting out of bed so that you can quickly write down your dreams.

2. Write the date at the top of the page, followed by everything you can remember about the dream. Always write in the present tense so that you can relive the dream at any time.

3. Identify any themes or specific details about the dream. For example, you might realize children were the theme or that you were at a favorite holiday destination. Identify any people, places, emotions, and sensory experiences from the dream.

4. Sketch any part of the dream that is particularly vivid, even if it is just a rough drawing or a quick map.

5. Add a title for the dream so that you can refer back to it easily. If it was a lucid dream, then add a large "L" next to the title, and try to determine what led to becoming lucid.

Recalling Your Dreams

Keeping a dream journal is your ticket to understanding your dreams, but you have to remember your dreams to write them down. Many people do not recall their dreams at all or only remember small fragments. You might need to work hard at recall before you can fill your journal. Recalling your dreams is important because you won't know you had a lucid dream if you cannot remember it. Additionally, recalling dreams increases your awareness of being in a dream the next time and allows you to familiarize yourself with your favorite dream worlds.

Try some of these tips to improve your dream recall:

- Get enough sleep so that your body can go through several REM cycles. The longer you sleep, the more REM cycles you have, which increases your chances of vivid dreams.
- Take time to fall asleep by relaxing or meditating for about 20 minutes before bed and readying your mind for dreaming. Falling asleep too quickly means you are sleep deprived, and that decreases your recall greatly.
- Wake up without an alarm clock so that your dreams are formed fully, then take some time to dwell on your dreams and write them down in your journal.
- Some people find a sleep supplement helpful to control brain waves and induce REM sleep. Not only will you sleep better, but you might also have more REM sleep and remember dreams more easily.

- Meditate on the phrase "I will recall my dreams," and you will program your mind to remember dreams over time.

- Drink several large glasses of water before going to bed. You will wake up to urinate throughout the night, and the most likely time to wake up is after a REM sleep cycle. Try to recall your dream immediately and write down a few short notes before going back to sleep, or simply recall your dream and write it down in the morning.

Dream recall includes all types of dreams and not just lucid dreaming. Potentially, you could remember all seven types of dreams. It is best to focus on recalling ordinary dreams first if you do not usually remember any dreams. To have a successful lucid dreaming experience, you need to remember at least one dream every night.

Catalog Your Dream Signs

A dream sign is anything that makes you realize that you are dreaming and that what you are seeing is not real. Dream signs help with reality checking and indicate a state of dreaming. Identifying your dream signs can alert you to your dream, which increases your awareness and opens you to lucid dreaming. An extra limb, walking through walls, or an odd plant in a familiar place are examples of dream signs. They might be quite obvious or something more personal to you.

Dr. LaBerge suggests four types of dream signs:

1. Inner awareness: You realize your thoughts, perceptions, sensations, or emotions are strange. For example, you might think about jumping and then start flying through the air.
2. Action: A physical activity by you, other characters, or objects is different from expectations. For example, you might be chopping vegetables and realize that you cannot stop the knife from moving along the chopping board, even as the blade reaches your fingers.
3. Form: The appearance of something, like a place, inanimate object, or person seems strange. For example, a person might have a third eye, or a building could be upside down.
4. Context: The situation you are in is unrealistic or impossible when compared to what you know as truth. For example, you are living in an underwater empire or taking part in tribal rituals on Saturn.

Look through your journal and the details of each dream. Try to find something that frequently appears or happens in your dreams, as those elements could be dream signs. Write them down and try to find them the next time you dream to help with becoming lucid.

Setting Goals for Lucid Dreaming

Anything you want to achieve in life requires hard work, dedication, and perseverance. One of the best ways to achieve things is to set goals because it gives you a plan to work towards. Lucid dreaming should be seen as a project, and you can set goals to achieve different levels of lucidity and induce lucid dreams.

Always create clear goals with explicit outcomes that you can measure against some benchmark. For example, start with goals to recall dreams. You might set a goal of remembering and writing down one dream per night. You can measure your achievements easily by checking if you wrote down one dream for each night. Later on, you could consider other goals, such as having one lucid dream per month.

Your goals should be realistic but challenging. Lucid dreaming is a challenge in itself, so try something specific like an action within a dream. For example, your goal might be to time travel in your dream or to face a fear. As you get more practice, challenge yourself more to do more difficult things while lucid dreaming.

Scheduling Lucid Dreaming Time

Setting goals for lucid dreaming can seem like a huge task if you are not accustomed to having them frequently. Some people move lucid dreaming to one side because they have some concerns or feel that a specific night isn't appropriate for lucid dreaming. But, you cannot improve your lucid dreaming skills if you do not have lucid dreams—you need to make time for them. You could schedule a time for lucid dreaming on weekends if you are worried they might interfere with your workday, or add lucid dreaming to each night.

The Cycle Adjustment Technique

One technique to increase the frequency of lucid dreaming is by using the Cycle Adjustment technique, known as CAT, by naturally altering the chemicals in your body. These chemical changes allow you to adjust your sleep cycles and increase REM consciousness. Some people have four lucid dreams per week by using this technique, and most people have success within their first two weeks of consistent practice.

CAT requires only two adjustments in your routine, but you have to go to bed at the same time every night. During the first week, set your alarm for 90 minutes earlier than your usual time to wake up. During the second week, alternate between waking at your normal time and then waking 90 minutes earlier the next day.

The first week of the CAT technique disrupts your internal clock and resets your body's sleep cycles. You should not have any lucid dreams in the first week because of this interruption. Lucid dreams could occur frequently in the second week when you are waking up at your normal time. Your body expects to wake up early, so mental awareness increases in the last 90 minutes of sleep and boosts your chances of lucid dreaming.

Wake Back to Bed Technique

The Wake Back to Bed, or WBTB technique, provides immediate lucid dreaming if you intentionally follow all the steps. Go to bed at your normal time and set your alarm to wake you in six hours. Get out of bed when your alarm rings and wake yourself up entirely, then get some mental stimulation for 20 to 60 minutes to increase your awareness. For example, read or build a puzzle. Finally, get back in bed and relax by meditating or using mnemonic stimulation techniques. Visualize yourself in the dreamscape and think about your lucid dream while falling asleep.

WBTB induces lucid dreaming because you stimulate your brain with activity while awake, and this occurs when you would have been in REM sleep. Mental stimulation enhances consciousness and plunges you back into REM sleep once you fall asleep, so you are more aware as you start to dream.

Attentive Relaxation

Lucid dreaming requires a person to relax and be attentive while asleep. Lucid dreaming techniques only work when you have attentive relaxation, but you have to learn methods to reach this state before you learn dream-inducing techniques. Attentive relaxation allows you to have an alert mind while your body goes into deep relaxation. Progressive relaxation and 61-point relaxation methods can help you with attentive relaxation, and you might be familiar with some of these techniques already.

Progressive Relaxation

This technique focuses on relaxing one muscle group at a time. It makes you aware of each part of your body and releases tension in each area. Spend time concentrating on each step before you move to the next one.

1. Sit or lie down in a comfortable position. Take five deep breaths by inhaling slowly through your nose and exhaling steadily through your mouth.

2. Concentrate on your toes and flex them upwards. Hold this position for a moment, then release the tension. Point your toes towards the

bottom and hold for a moment, then release them slowly.

3. Tense the muscles of your calves and hold for a few seconds, then release the tension slowly.

4. Scrunch your knees together for a moment, then release.

5. Tense your thigh muscles and hold the position, then release.

6. Clench your hands into fists focusing on the tension, then open your hands.

7. Squeeze your arm muscles and release.

8. Squeeze your buttocks together for a few moments and release.

9. Pull in your abdominal muscles for a few seconds, then release them slowly.

10. Inhale while tensing your chest and hold your breath for a few counts before exhaling as you release tension.

11. Scrunch your shoulders towards your ears and hold the position, then lower them as you relax.

12. Purse your lips together in a pout and hold, then return to a neutral position slowly.

13. Open your mouth as wide as possible and feel the stretch in your jaw, then return to a normal position.

14. Scrunch your eyes closed and hold for a moment before releasing the muscles.

15. Raise your eyebrows to scrunch your forehead and release after a few moments.
16. Finish by taking a few deep breaths.

61-Point Relaxation

This technique requires a person to concentrate on 61 different points in the body. You can focus on each point by counting it or imagining a blue star as it travels from point-to-point. The amount of time you spend at each point is up to you, so try a few different methods. Some people inhale while moving from one point to another and exhale once they reach the point since exhaling is more relaxing. Alternatively, forget about how you are breathing and simply count out a few seconds on each point while breathing normally.

Spend some time to relax each point in the following order:

1. Center of your forehead
2. Front of the neck
3. Right shoulder
4. Right elbow
5. Right wrist
6. Right thumb
7. Right index finger
8. Right middle finger
9. Right ring finger
10. Right little finger

11. Right wrist
12. Right elbow
13. Right shoulder
14. Front of the neck
15. Left shoulder
16. Left elbow
17. Left wrist
18. Left thumb
19. Left index finger
20. Left middle finger
21. Left ring finger
22. Left little finger
23. Left wrist
24. Left elbow
25. Left shoulder
26. Front of the neck
27. Center of chest
28. Right of chest
29. Center of chest
30. Left of chest
31. Center of chest
32. Naval
33. Pubic bone
34. Right hip
35. Right knee
36. Right ankle
37. Right big toe
38. Right second toe

39. Right third toe
40. Right fourth toe
41. Right little toe
42. Right ankle
43. Right knee
44. Right hip
45. Pubic bone
46. Left hip
47. Left knee
48. Left ankle
49. Left big toe
50. Left second toe
51. Left third toe
52. Left fourth toe
53. Left little toe
54. Left ankle
55. Left knee
56. Left hip
57. Pubic bone
58. Navel
59. Center of chest
60. Front of neck
61. Center of forehead

Schedule enough time to practice relaxation techniques. You will require some time to learn each method, especially the different steps or points, so the exercises might not feel relaxing the first few times. As you practice more, the techniques become effortless, and you enhance your relaxation.

Meditation for Lucid Dreaming

Meditation is a great way to improve your mindfulness and increase your awareness of yourself. It allows you to destress and releases built-up tension in your muscles. It improves concentration and encourages abstract thinking. The following two meditation techniques can help you with lucid dreaming. You can try one or both techniques, and some people practice these techniques back-to-back.

Breathing Meditation

A breathing meditation helps to calm a person's mind. It is a meditation you should practice daily and works well as a quick stress reliever when your day becomes frantic. Find a quiet place to sit down, like on the floor or in a chair, and ensure your back remains straight.

Close your eyes and take note of your breathing. Just breathe naturally and feel how the air moves through your body as you inhale and exhale. Your mind may become full of thoughts but do not entertain them. All you should be doing is focusing on your breathing. Refocus yourself every time your mind wanders until your mind is calm. Aim to practice breathing meditation for 10 to 15 minutes.

Guided Meditation

This meditation takes place in a beautiful garden that you will create in your mind. It allows you to concentrate, increase your awareness, and boost your creativity. Focus on letting go of any anxiety during the meditation and do not dwell on other thoughts. Your concentration should be on visualization to such an extent that it feels as if your mind separates from your body. This meditation takes at least 15 minutes for full awareness, but you can meditate for as long as you want.

Sit comfortably in a quiet area and close your eyes while breathing normally. Imagine that a beautiful garden surrounds you—it is full of magnificent trees and shrubs, colorful flowers, interesting plants, maybe a waterfall, and lots of animal life. Concentrate on breathing in the fresh air of the garden as you look around. Explore the garden with all your senses by smelling flowers, feeling different plants or the grass, or picking fruit to eat from a tree. Listen to the birds chirping and let a butterfly settle on your hand. Once you are ready to return to your reality, count backward from five while breathing deeply and then open your eyes slowly.

You now have all the tools to prepare yourself for lucid dreaming. Use everything you learned in this chapter to increase your awareness and improve your consciousness while you are awake and while you are sleeping. These tools will help you to experience dreams more readily and prepare you for inducing lucid dreaming.

Chapter 4:

Dream From Within The Dream

A variety of techniques can help you to train yourself to lucid dream. Some of these techniques are suitable for beginners while others are more challenging. In the following two chapters, we will look at these techniques to stimulate dreams.

These induction techniques will help you to:

- Recall dreams better
- Improve sensory experiences while dreaming
- Realize you are dreaming (lucidity)
- Increase your self-awareness while you are awake
- Increase your self-awareness while you are asleep
- Develop visualization skills
- Program your dream narrative before falling asleep

Use these methods as a basic guideline and determine which ones work best for you. Focus on observations, exploration, and stepping out of your comfort zone. Many lucid dreamers develop their own methods that could be a combination of techniques, so persevere and you will succeed.

Performing Reality Checks

Reality checks help you to know whether you are awake or in a dream. It is a technique that encourages lucid dreaming, but you should only attempt it if you have several dream signs and journal frequently. Reality checking helps to increase your self-awareness while you are awake and assists when you are asleep.

Reality checking alerts you to being in a dream. Quite simply, it is noticing that what you are experiencing is not real and that you are dreaming. You can only know you are in a dream if you compare your dream with reality when you are awake, so you need to practice reality checking constantly.

How to Do Reality Checking

To realize you are dreaming, you need to have a definite test consisting of two parts. You could answer a basic question and execute a predetermined action that is impossible in real life. Doing these two tests ensures that you have a backup if one of them fails. You could even do more tests, and with time, you will find the ones that work best for your reality or dream state.

The tests you choose should be done while you are awake and get a conclusive answer for each test. Doing reality checking while awake programs these tests into your mind for when you are sleeping. Do each of your chosen tests at least ten times while you are awake, and these tests will show up in your dreams where you can test them again. Once you realize your reality check failed, you are set to continue with lucid dreaming.

Ideas for Reality Checking

Some ideas for questions:

- Am I dreaming?
- Is this image/object before me real? Does it disappear if I look away or blink?
- Ask yourself a basic math question, for example: what is 2+2?
- Does the time of my watch agree with the color of the sky outside?
- Does any part of my body look strange?

"Impossible" actions to try:

- Push your fingers on one hand through the palm of the other hand.

- Check if you can breathe while holding your nose and mouth closed.
- Push your hand or fist through a hard surface (like a wall).
- Try to fly or float.
- Determine if any of your senses is better or worse (like seeing without glasses).

Each person has their own reality checks that work for them, so the ideas above should serve as an inspiration. Look back in your dream journal and at your dream signs. These dream signs are ideal for reality checking because they can speed up the testing process. Ensure you are fully aware of these signs and practice additional reality checking to strengthen your abilities.

Combine your dream signs and reality checks to help you stay aware while dreaming. Reality checks assist in remaining lucid. Whenever you find yourself drifting off, do a reality check and then ground yourself by saying, "I am dreaming. I am lucid." Grounding is essential if you want your lucid dreams to last longer.

Lucid Dream Intentions

Previously, we spoke about setting goals for lucid dreaming; now, start focusing on setting goals for your lucid dreams. This "goal" is called a lucid dream intention, and it is something you want to achieve while in the dream state. It could be something as simple as talking to a specific person in your dream or an intricate intention with detailed planning. Lucid dream intentions can be used with many inducing techniques and work well with the Mnemonic Induction of Lucid Dreams (MILD) technique.

Dream intentions help you to control the narrative while lucid dreaming. For example, you might plan a list of questions or talking points for the person you want to speak to. You could plan it in more detail, like imagining the scenery around you during the chat, what you will wear, how you will move from one place to another, and even what the weather will be. Use your dream intentions to spark your creativity and encourage lucid dreaming.

The MILD Technique

The MILD technique is perfect for beginners as it induces lucid dreams quickly. Any mnemonic is a learning tool that improves your memory. MILD is a technique by Dr. LaBerge and it was found to give instant results. It focuses on enhancing self-awareness to identify dreaming, reciting affirmations to remain lucid, and stating dream intentions to encourage lucidity.

The first two steps of MILD are done while awake and the rest while you are in bed. Schedule enough time to complete each step and relax while you are doing them.

1. Recall Your Dreams

By now, you should have remembered (at least one per night) and written down many dreams. Aim to recall your dreams in great detail; otherwise, your chances of lucid dreaming are low. By recalling dreams, you are aiding mnemonic memory.

2. Do Reality Checks Throughout the Day

Frequently question whether you are asleep or dreaming. You can set a timer for every hour to perform your checks during the day. The most important thing is to know the difference in answer to reality checks when you are awake versus when asleep.

3. Recite Affirmations About Lucidity

An affirmation is a positive thing a person says to help program mnemonic memory and encourage action—for example, looking in the mirror and saying, "I am beautiful," until you start believing it. Affirmations for lucid dreaming include: "I will remember my dreams. I am lucid dreaming tonight. I am dreaming now." Repeat them constantly for a few minutes until you are on the edge of falling asleep.

4. Visualize Your Dreams

Start visualizing your dream as you are about to fall asleep and when you are very relaxed. Recall a recent dream but know that the ending will change. Visualize the dream in great detail and try to find a dream sign. Once you identify a sign, state, "I'm dreaming!" Currently, you are only daydreaming, but continue with the visualization and setting dream intentions. Do everything as if it is a lucid dream.

It is quite likely that you will fall asleep during the visualization process. This is fine because you want your final waking memory to be about lucid dreaming. The likelihood of having a lucid dream in a later stage of sleep increases, and you could become lucid spontaneously. The MILD technique is an ideal companion to the WBTB method described in the previous chapter, so wake up for some time and get mental stimulation before returning to bed.

Tholey's Combined Technique

Tholey's Combined Technique usually gives better results than MILD but it takes quite some time. Try this technique over a weekend or while on holiday when you have more time available.

1. Reflection

Ask yourself, "Am I dreaming?" a minimum of five times each day. Imagine you are in a dream while asking this question and experience everything—your surroundings and body—as if it was a dream. While thinking about this question, consider events that took place recently and in the past, and try to identify any strange elements in your memory. Ask this reflective question whenever you feel a situation seems unrealistic or dream-like or if you see a specific dream sign.

2. *Intention*

Sometimes, your dreams contain ideas or narratives that have nothing to do with your daily life or that you rarely experience while awake—for example, flying, spinning, or playing an instrument. Concentrate on these things while you are awake and imagine yourself experiencing these events. Use all your senses to focus on "doing" the task, even if it seems impossible. Continuously tell yourself you are dreaming during this visualization. Use memory recall techniques if you struggle to remember your dream details since this information helps with visualization.

3. *Auto-Suggestion*

Do not push the idea of lucid dreaming once you get in bed; rather, focus on being aware when dreaming. Decide on an action you want to do while dreaming to auto-suggest a dream. Maintaining consciousness while drifting into sleep can be challenging, so try one of these techniques as you fall asleep:

- Focus only on visualization (imagery).
- Concentrate on your body, such as breathing and relaxing muscles.

- Pay attention to both visualization and your body.
- Become an ego-point where you perceive everything from a specific point in the dream world.
- Concentrate on imagery from the ego-point.

The time-consuming nature of this method forces you to become more aware and could be the reason for its effectiveness.

The DILD Method

The Dream Induced Lucid Dreaming technique (DILD) occurs when you suddenly become lucid in a dream. Unrealistic elements in your dream alert you to your dream state and make you lucid. Reality testing is one of the best ways to induce lucidity, so always ask, "Am I dreaming?" when you see something unusual in your dream.

There are many ways to encourage a DILD, including:

- Using the Cycle Adjustment technique
- Identifying dream signs
- Setting dream intentions and meditating
- Using the Wake Back To Bed method
- Performing reality checks

Most people experience lucid dreams as a result of the DILD technique. It is something you could experience without even realizing you triggered consciousness in some way. Many individuals find that DILD becomes a routine practice and almost consider themselves as natural lucid dreamers.

The DEILD Method

The DEILD method, or Dream Exit Induced Lucid Dream, allows you to slide from being awake into a lucid dream. It can be a hassle-free method if the conditions are right, and you can create a dream chain by using this technique several times throughout the night. This technique also helps to reenter a dream if you woke up too quickly so that you can continue the experience.

1. Wake Briefly

To start a DEILD, you have to wake up briefly. The ideal time is after four to six hours of sleep. Light sleepers frequently wake up during the night, so DEILD is a suitable technique for effortless use. Heavier sleepers may have some trouble with waking up naturally for DEILD; use a lucid dreaming app or alarm clock to wake you up briefly during REM sleep. The alarm should get you out of your dream state, but you mustn't become fully awake, and the alarm should switch itself off to cause less disruption.

2. *Remain Still and Visualize*

Lie still once you reach the area between dreaming and being awake as you don't want to alert your motor functions to being awake. If you move, then you become fully conscious since your neurons start sending signals through your brain and body. Moving will also cause sleep paralysis to wear off, which you don't want to happen. Your eyes should remain closed as you lie still.

Recall the dream you just experienced and imagine yourself back in the space you were before you woke up. This process might happen effortlessly, or it could take a few moments if you have to recall your sensory experience during your dream.

3. *Reenter the Dream*

Reentering your previous dream should occur if you followed the previous steps correctly. The amazing thing is that you can now have a lucid dream even if you were having an ordinary dream before waking up. Do a reality check when you enter the dream.

Lucid dreams induced with this technique are vivid because you are increasing your awareness. You reenter the dream with full lucidity so you can visualize and add on to the existing narrative. The entire DEILD process should only take a couple of seconds. If you are awake for any longer, then your ability to reenter the dream reduces drastically.

The FILD Method

Finger Induced Lucid Dreaming (FILD) is an interesting technique to try if you have mastered the basics of lucid dreaming. This method is something to try if you haven't had a lucid dream in a while. It is super easy to learn, but you will need some daytime practice to get it just right.

1. *Practice During the Day*

Practice the finger movement for FILD during the day so that you can master this technique when you are in bed. Choose any two fingers, like the index and middle finger, and alternate between moving them up and down. If your one finger is up, then the other should be down, almost like tapping out a rhythm. Make the movements as small as possible—your fingers shouldn't be moving more than a tiny fraction of an inch at any time. Concentrate on establishing a solid connection between your mind and body while doing this movement.

2. *Find the Right Time*

The FILD technique works optimally when a person is exhausted. You really want to be tired enough that you could fall asleep within a minute or so after lying down. The best time could be after waking up during the night, like when you need a drink of water or to use the restroom. Alternatively, set an alarm to ring in about four to six hours and then use FILD to get back to sleep.

3. *Put FILD in Place*

Relax in bed once you find the best (most tired) time for FILD. Don't worry about visualization or following instructions—simply relax. Start the finger movement once you feel yourself starting to fall asleep. You have practiced this movement already, so it will establish a connection between brain and body. Continue moving your fingers for about 30 seconds as you relax more.

Do a reality check, like pushing your fingers through your other hand, to see if you are dreaming. If you can do an impossible action, then you are in a lucid dream. Of course, this attempt might not have been successful, and you are still awake. In this case, it is best to fall asleep naturally and try the technique another night.

Reality checks are very important during FILD, so ensure you perform them frequently throughout the day. Practice the finger movements and only use this technique if you are tired. The last thing you want is having to concentrate on the movement when you are almost asleep. Get the technique down before attempting it at night.

Self-Hypnosis

Self-hypnosis is similar to relaxation and meditation techniques but differs as your brain enters a trance. It helps you understand your emotions and thoughts better and is not at all like the mockery you see performed by hypnotists on stage. Self-hypnosis improves your self-awareness, and you maintain full control of your mind and body. You cannot get stuck in a trance and will come out of it naturally. Hypnosis makes you more suggestible because endorphins are released, which allows you to auto-suggest lucid dreaming.

1. Find a Comfortable Spot

Sit or lie down in a comfortable area. You should have an open posture—don't cross your arms or legs. Ensure you are comfortable as this process takes about 20 minutes. Close your eyes gently and take three deep breaths. Ensure you inhale and feel your chest expanding. Release any anxiety and tension as you exhale. Notice your thoughts but let them go past without interacting or dwelling on any topic.

2. *Release All Tension*

Release all the physical tension caught in your body. Start with your toes and move up your body to relax each muscle group. Imagine each area of your body melting away until only warm relaxation is left. Only move to the next muscle if your current muscle group is relaxed fully. Your upper back, shoulders, neck, and jaw may require even more concentration as they store a lot of tension.

3. *Visualize*

Visualize a staircase. You are standing at the very top of the staircase. This image is a representation of your consciousness. Start climbing down the stairs using one step at a time and feel yourself drifting deeper into a relaxed trance state. Keep your body very still and try to roll your eyes back gently. You can also count the stairs as you descend but start counting up from 10.

4. Make Auto-Suggestions

Start making auto-suggestions when you are at the bottom of the staircase. Each auto-suggestion should be in the present tense and positive. Repeat your chosen auto-suggestions (one or a few) several times. Try the following auto-suggestions or write your own:

- I can recall my dreams.
- I am aware of my surroundings.
- I control my dreams.
- I can have lucid dreams.

5. Exit Slowly

Recite the auto-suggestion as many times as you like and enjoy this relaxed state. Feel the waves of positivity rolling over you. Create an image of you reaching your goal. Alert yourself once you are ready to wake up or exit the trance. Clearly state that you are going to count to 10 and awareness will increase with every step. Start at the bottom of the staircase and take the first step as you count. Inhale deeply once you are at the top of the stairs and open your eyes. Remain in this position for a few moments then stand up slowly.

Some people struggle with the idea of self-hypnosis and need some more help to get the hang of it. You can make a voice recording that guides you through each step and follow your recorded instructions if that is better for you. Alternatively, download a self-hypnosis recording, such as those in hypnosis apps, and follow the given instructions. During the night, your mind will use the thoughts you anchored during hypnosis and possibly induce a lucid dream.

Stimulate Lucid Dreams With Five Types of Dreams

There are many types of dreams, and classifications vary greatly. Each categorization depends on a specific thing a person is analyzing, for example, what a person dreams about or the time of night a dream occurs. With this in mind, let's consider five types of dreams that most of us are familiar with and can use to encourage lucid dreaming.

Daydreams

Did you know that most people daydream for one to two hours per day? That is a lot of time in a dream state! Daydreaming becomes a hypnotic activity, and it could be difficult to simply snap out of it. You are not asleep, but the reality is murky too, so it is a semi-sleep/semi-awake state.

Daydreaming starts with a basic idea that you explore as you get deeper into your own thoughts. It links closely to visualization during lucid dreams, so daydream away. Both the MILD and Wake Induced Lucid Dream (WILD, which we'll cover in Chapter 5) techniques use daydreaming (visualization) in their steps. Use your time daydreaming to set dream intentions, and see yourself achieving different goals. The more you visualize an event, the more likely it is to appear in a lucid dream.

Ordinary Dreams

These are normal dreams that everyone has and mostly occur during REM sleep. You probably dream about 100 minutes each night but seldom remember all your dreams. A large proportion of normal dreams occur from unconscious thoughts. You want to bring the focus to consciousness if you plan on lucid dreaming.

Normal dreams can become lucid at any time; all you need to do is become aware that you are dreaming. Ordinary dreams are used during the DILD technique to start lucidity. You can attempt to do reality checks while sleeping or simply acknowledge you are dreaming, and you may enter lucidity.

Lucid Dreams

Lucid dreams are part of the five types of dreams you may experience. A lucid dream occurs anytime that you become aware of dreaming and can control aspects of your dream. Extend your lucid dream by changing the direction it is taking or by constructing elaborate dream plots ahead of time.

False Awakenings

A false awakening is a type of dream inside a dream. You wake up and go ahead with your day just like you always do, only to realize a few moments later that you are still dreaming. False awakenings are vivid and feel extremely real unless you can do a reality check or realize in some way that you are still dreaming, like having a spouse when you are a single person.

False awakenings can be a single occurrence or repeat several times before waking up for real. It is a huge indicator to do more reality checks in the morning once you wake up. If you do reality checks while awake, then you can identify false awakenings more easily while asleep and catapult into lucid dreaming since you have more awareness.

Nightmares

A nightmare is a scary dream originating from an ordinary dream. You have no idea you are dreaming, so it feels very real. Nightmares can occur naturally or be a result of illness, alcohol, drugs, or trauma. Although nightmares are frightening, you can find a moment somewhere to become lucid and realize you are dreaming.

Lucid dreaming from nightmares can happen if you have a shocking experience that makes you lucid. For example, you might be running away from a monster and screaming, "Get away from me!" or are about to be beheaded and shout, "Wake up!" As soon you exclaim something of this nature, it shows that you are aware something is not real or irrational. Most people wake up at this point, but you should rather take a moment after this exclamation to realize you are dreaming and change the direction of the dream.

The techniques in this chapter are great for beginner and intermediate lucid dreamers. Try each one several times to find ones that work for you. Do reality checks constantly throughout the day and set dream intentions to encourage lucid dreaming. Try to become more aware while dreaming and use all kinds of dreams to increase your lucidity.

Chapter 5:

Consciously Falling Asleep

In the previous chapter, we looked at how you can induce lucid dreams by implanting ideas from the waking world into your dreams. This chapter is slightly different because we will look at how you can enter a lucid dream from a waking state. This process involves remaining aware (conscious) while falling asleep and entering a lucid dream immediately.

Hypnagogic Imagery

In the period between being awake and falling asleep, your consciousness is in a transitional state called hypnagogia. During this phase, you might have hypnagogic experiences that include imagery, sounds, and movements, like muscle twitches. These involuntary experiences are hypnagogic hallucinations.

Most people experience hypnagogia in some form, and you might notice that you already had hypnagogic imagery. Hypnagogia might start with seeing flashing images, almost like stars, or vivid kaleidoscopic pictures that start to move as you transition further into sleep. If you remain aware, then the imagery could become three-dimensional, and you feel immersed in it. This is a doorway to a lucid dream and very helpful for the next induction technique.

The WILD Method

The Wake Induced Lucid Dream (WILD) technique is a more complex method whereby a person enters a lucid dream state directly from the waking state. WILD is fantastic because you can become lucid when you want and experience a vivid dream with peak lucidity. This is an intuitive method with origins in Tibetan dream yoga. It requires knowledge about your body's sleep signals and responses.

With the WILD method, your mind remains conscious when your body falls asleep. You should be very relaxed when using this technique, so it might be best to try it if you take a lucid dreaming supplement. The other option is to use the WILD technique if you wake up after four to six because you will be in a very relaxed state.

2. Relax

Lie in bed just like you would normally so that you can relax your body entirely. Most people find the corpse position is best when doing this technique. Lie on your back with your arms at your sides, palms facing up, and with your legs straight. Other sleep positions work too but can cut off circulation to parts of your body, which causes you to wake up or prevents you from relaxing fully.

Close your eyes gently and stare into the back of your eyelids. Clear your mind of all thoughts by simply acknowledging them and letting go. Take ten slow, deep breaths by using the following pattern: Inhale for four counts, hold your breath for seven counts, and exhale for eight counts.

3. Experience Hypnagogia

Hypnagogic imagery will start to appear as you enter a relaxed state. Notice the luminous patterns crossing over your field of vision. Immerse yourself fully in their brightness and movement to increase your awareness. If you do not experience hypnagogia, then press your palms lightly over your eyes for about 20 seconds to induce imagery.

Continue to remain aware as your body falls asleep. Flow with the hypnagogia or look into the distance behind it and into the dream world. Continuously repeat the affirmation, "I am dreaming." Your mind could start playing tricks on you to fall asleep, so repeat the affirmation to maintain consciousness. As your body falls asleep, you could experience sleep paralysis, strange sounds, or the illusion of movement. At this stage, you might feel as if your mind is separate from your body.

4. Imagine Your Dream World

The dream world could be flashing in and out of your mind at this point. Now is the time to create your dream world and initiate your lucid dream. There are two ways to enter the dream world, and you can use either one. Sometimes, you have a choice in the matter; other times, your body and mind choose for you.

a. With Visualization

The first way to construct your dream scene is through visualization. Start imagining your dream scene and add different layers to make it vivid. Think about every detail of the landscape and everything in it. Add colors, sounds, sights, smells, and anything else your heart desires. Once your dream world is alive, place yourself in the center of it and become fully aware of your surroundings. Start moving around and interacting with elements in your dream world.

Leave your physical body behind as you move further into your dream. Consider yourself as only being a part of the dream and not anything else. Let your body sleep while you inhibit a lucid body created in your mind. Perform a reality check and then enjoy your lucidity fully while your body sleeps.

b.   With an Out-of-Body Exit

Hypnagogic imagery can be intoxicating and put you into a deeply relaxed state before you can use visualization to create a dream world. In this case, your awareness defaults to your bedroom. The difference, though, is that it is a dream bedroom. It can be very difficult to distinguish between your real and dream room but look around for small differences, and you will realize it is a dream.

Once you reach this state, you are already in a lucid dream but not the dream you want to be in. You could experience vibrations, which sound like a buzzing in your ears, or the illusion of shivering. Sleep paralysis is likely in this case too, which can be scary if you thought you were in a lucid dream.

To get out of your lucid dream bedroom, you will need to get out of your body. Some people manage to do this by imagining they are getting out of bed and leaving their physical body for a dream body in that way. Sometimes, your body will fight against this idea of movement because of sleep paralysis, so you need another way out. Try to sink, float, or swing out of your body. For example, imagine you are floating in a pool and your dream body drifts away from your physical body, or imagine you are on a swing moving backward and forwards then jump off it to leave your body, or imagine how your dream body sinks into your bed. Use this out-of-body momentum to launch yourself into a dream.

If you cannot get out of your body in one of these ways, then use teleportation to move to somewhere else. You are lucid dreaming already, so take control of your surroundings. Make a clear statement about where you want to be, like saying, "I am going to the Caribbean right now." You should be able to change locations in this way and leave your physical body behind as you continue further into your dream.

WILD is not easy to do, so practice frequently. Many people fall asleep before they finish step two, and you might have to practice each step on its own several times before adding them all together in sequence. Only about half of WILD attempts are successful. Don't give up; try again in a few days' time. A WILD is an amazing experience with great vividness, but you need to be entirely relaxed, maintain conscious awareness, and go with the flow.

Lucidity Through Visualization

Visualization is one of the best ways to become lucid while dreaming. Traditionally, visualization refers to imagining a scene in visual (sight) terms. For lucid dreaming, you should take visualization even further and consider it a multi-sensory activity. There are many ways to encourage visualization—try some or all of them to improve your visualization skills.

A Tibetan Doctrine

The Tibetans consider the dream state as the third doctrine within six yoga doctrines. Yoga is a type of teaching and not just the physical exercise form. This method is quite complex and consists of a host of smaller activities and beliefs. It is something you can look into more if Tibetan methods intrigue you. For the purpose of this book, I will briefly summarize the Tibetan doctrine for the dream state, and some of these elements are discussed in the following sections.

The dream state is split into four parts that improve lucidity. It should help you to visualize better and improve your lucid dreams.

- The first part of the doctrine is related to comprehending (understanding) your dream state. This comprehension comes from the Power of Resolution, the Power of Breath, and the Power of Visualization. There are various skills and techniques within each power to increase awareness.

- The second part is transmuting the dream, whereby you take control of the dream content and focus on the mind as a source of power.

- Realizing the dream state is the third part and includes dream content. In this part, the dreamer recognizes the dream and its contents as transformational and similar to a deity.

- The final part is meditating on "thatness," which is the reasoning behind the dream. It allows you to experience greater awareness and creates an illusory effect in waking and sleeping.

Tibetan White Dot Visualization

The Tibetan White Dot technique forms part of the Tibetan doctrine on the dream state. It is a relatively easy visualization method that you can use at any time. This method requires some attention before going to sleep and additional input at dawn or when you wake up.

c.   Before Bed

Make a resolution that you are going to recognize your dream state. Use the throat chakra for visualization. Do this by sounding the syllable "ah" from your throat and visualize a radiant red color. Focus on the radiating energy of "ah" and imagine the dream world illuminating around you.

d. *When You Wake Up*

Take several deep breaths and feel your stomach extend as the air enters your body. Resolve to recognize and understand your dream state eleven times. Next, imagine a white dot in between your eyebrows and concentrate on this spot until you enter a dream state.

Tibetan Black Dot Visualization

The black dot method is another aspect of Tibetan doctrine. It requires knowledge of the white dot technique for the period before you go to bed, so ensure you practice the above steps before moving to this method.

e. *Before Bed*

Imagine a white dot in the area between your eyebrows. Concentrate on it in such a way that it becomes a meditation.

f. *When You Wake Up*

Take 21 slow, deep breaths and resolve to recognize your dream with every breath. Next, imagine a black dot located at the root chakra, which is found at the base of the spine in the pelvic region. Concentrate on this black dot until you enter a dream state.

Multisensory Visualization

Superb visualization requires the utilization of all your senses. Start your visualization by focusing on hypnagogia. Let the colors flow freely in front of your eyes until it takes over your mind's eye. Now, use these hypnagogic colors to create a landscape of your choosing. Most people have a default landscape when practicing lucid dreaming techniques, like a tranquil garden or beach. Next, use all your senses to strengthen your dream scene.

g. See

The first sense you will use is your sight to create the visual landscape. Imagine the horizon of your dream scene and add some lines to distinguish between different areas of the landscape. Add more details to your landscape, like clouds in the sky or pebbles on the ground. Ensure you give color to your dream even if everything is still in black and white. Focus on each object until its color appears. Add as many details to your scene as you wish. Try to visualize things far away in the dream and then bring your attention closer to you by looking at what is around your feet or within reach.

h. Hear

Listen for sounds in your landscape or place them within the dream if you cannot hear anything. You might start by placing the sound of birds in your garden and then listen intently for other sounds. Soon, you could hear crickets chirping, the rush of a waterfall, or the wind rustling through the leaves.

i. Touch

Walk around your dream landscape and touch different things. Start by focusing on what is underneath your feet. It might be a cold metal floor or the sand between your toes on the beach. Find an element in your dream scene and run your hands over it, like petting a puppy or picking a flower and feeling its petals. Pay attention to how your skin feels in your dream. It could be hot because the sun is shining, or you might feel the spray of a waterfall dusting your face.

j. Smell

Your olfactory sense can give a strong feeling of awareness within your dreamscape. Inhale deeply through your nose and try to identify the smells around you. If you cannot smell anything, then place specific smell ideas in your landscape. For example, you might place the smell of pine trees if you are surrounded by a forest or the smell of coconuts and pineapples while in the tropics. Walk through the landscape and smell as many elements as possible to induce more olfactory awareness.

k. *Taste*

Gustatory visualization refers to imagining tastes in your dream. If there is something in your dream that you know should have a taste, then head over to that element and taste it. For example, pick a tomato from a vine and take a big bite, then focus on what it tastes like. Otherwise, think of a memory with a taste that you associate with a dreamscape. You might think about the sweet, sticky taste of s'mores if your dream scene is a campground or taste a cold tropical pina colada while lounging on the beach.

Using all your senses allows you to create a more intricate dream scene for improved immersion. It also boosts your awareness as you are more cognizant of changes in your environment, whether it be real or a dream scene.

Twin Bodies Technique

The twin bodies method provides a similar experience to the out-of-body exit. It focuses on leaving your physical body behind while entering a dream in a lucid body. This technique is best suited when you wake up during the night.

l. **Relax**

Start relaxing as soon as you wake up during the night. Keep your eyes closed while lying on your back or right side. Take deep breaths while focusing on relaxation. Tighten all the muscles in your body, then release them. Let go of any thoughts that come to the surface so that your mind remains clear. Repeat affirmations that set your dream intentions.

m. **Concentrate on Your Physical Body**

Take your time to concentrate on different parts of your body and notice the movements in that body part. Search for any strange sensations, like vibrations, and focus on that sensation. You should experience sleep paralysis shortly after noticing these sensations, which means you are ready for the next step.

n. **Leave Your Physical Body to Enter the Dream**

Plan to exit your physical body once sleep paralysis sets in. You can now enter your dream body, which is a twin to your physical body. Your dream body can move around—enter it by swinging, rolling, or flying out of your physical body. Use any method that works for you to enter your dream body.

Some people wake up as soon as they try to move into a dream body. Prevent this premature awakening by doing reality checks as soon as you are in a lucid dream. Continue to do reality checks throughout the dream so that your awareness does not wane. Use your different senses to experience your dream and remain lucid.

Counting Yourself to Sleep

Many people joke about counting sheep until they fall asleep, but you can actually use counting to stimulate lucid dreams. Start by lying comfortably in bed and relaxing entirely. Gently close your eyes and take deep breaths. Observe any thoughts that pop up and let them go again so that your mind becomes clear. Start counting by saying, "1, I am dreaming," and continue counting and repeating "I am dreaming" after every count. It helps you to remain aware while falling asleep and reaffirms you are dreaming when you enter a dream state. Start again from 1 if you reach 100 before you start to dream.

Visualization is an essential skill if you want to have vivid lucid dreams. The WILD technique induces the most spectacular and intricate lucid dreams, but you have to possess strong visualization skills. Strengthen your visualization skills during the day and before bed so that you can use them when asleep.

Sleep Posture and Lucid Dreaming

Every person has bedtime rituals, including a favorite sleeping position. How do you fall asleep or sleep throughout the night? Sometimes, you fall asleep in a specific position and wake up to pins and needles in a limb because the blood flow was minimal. These types of uncomfortable positions can prevent you from dreaming. You need to find the best way to be comfortable and dream.

The most prevalent sleeping positions are:

- Corpse: flat on your back with your legs straight and arms by your sides
- Fetus: arms and knees are bent and curled in towards the body like a baby in a womb
- Log: lying on your side with arms straight next to your body and legs extending down (like a ruler)
- Yearner: lying on your side with your arms extending in front of you (similar to the letter "r")
- Free-faller: lying on your stomach with your arms next to your head as if you are falling from the sky
- Starfish: lying on your back with arms and legs spread outwards

There is no right or wrong position for sleeping. You have to find the best position for you that ensures you get quality rest while giving you an opportunity to lucid dream. The corpse pose is a popular position for lucid dreaming because it does not limit blood flow to any limbs. It is useful for the WILD technique and helps you relax fully. Your natural sleeping position may promote lucid dreams, too, since you are in a relaxed state and comfortable in bed.

Lucid Dreaming Mistakes to Avoid

There are so many ways to encourage lucid dreaming that I am sure you will find at least one that will work for you! Sometimes, dream enthusiasts get overeager or make small mistakes that prevent or interrupt their lucid dreams. Being aware of these potential mistakes can help you to identify them in your practices and improve your dream experience.

Not Committing Fully

Some people try to lucid dream for a few nights and then give up if they do not succeed. Honestly, you need to give it a lot more time! Lucid dreaming doesn't happen at the snap of your fingers—it takes time and patience. Some of the techniques require more than two weeks just to get your mind ready for the process. Not a single day spent on preparing for lucid dreaming is a waste because you are becoming more aware and setting intentions. These are all good things, so remain committed and continue to try until you start lucid dreaming.

Overexertion

Sometimes people try too hard to have a lucid dream. They crave one so badly that they attempt various inducing techniques to no avail. It is important to focus on one technique at a time and focus only on that method; do not become scatterbrained and try everything at once. Do not rush techniques; rather, spend enough time on each one and practice, practice, practice. You cannot force a lucid dream, so relax and go to sleep. Focus more on relaxation and becoming aware instead of just lucid dreaming. You might surprise yourself and find dreams come easier when you don't try so hard.

Sleep Deprivation

Sleep deprivation occurs when a person doesn't get enough quality sleep. You could be experiencing poor sleep due to insomnia, stress, anxiety, or waking up frequently during the night. Lucid dreaming won't cause sleep deprivation, but your sleeping and dream-inducing habits could be a contributor. If an alarm wakes you in the morning, then you are disrupting your natural sleep cycle and potentially missing out on REM sleep. It is much better to wake up naturally because then your body has sufficient rest. Another issue is alarms set to wake you up for inducing dreams. If you set too many or remain awake instead of falling asleep, then you are getting too little sleep.

Insufficient Dream Recall

Lucid dreaming works at its best when you can recall your dreams. Dream recall is at the foundation of lucid dreaming because remembering and writing down your dreams helps you identify your dream signs. It also allows you to go back to a previous dream through visualization. Ensure you remember at least one dream every morning before inducing lucid dreaming.

Stabilization Problems

Stabilizing your dream includes immersing yourself in the scenery and remaining calm while doing reality checks. Many beginners become so excited about being lucid that they constantly exclaim, "I'm dreaming!" and dive headfirst into the experience to such an extent that they actually wake up. Yes, lucid dreaming is exciting, but you need to take all the necessary steps to avoid waking up.

Losing Lucidity

You can stop being lucid once you are in a lucid dream, which leaves you back in an ordinary dream. Usually, this happens when you are so immersed in the dream that you forget it is not real. The best way to remain lucid is to do a reality check frequently to remind yourself you are dreaming.

Being Overeager

Some lucid dreamers create major intentions and goals for their dreams, like wanting to fly or meet a specific celebrity. They become frustrated when their dream does not deliver these results and may feel lucid dreaming is a fallacy because they have limited control. Start small. You first need to improve your awareness and understand your dream world before you can set bigger goals. For example, flying might require you to start running first, and then you take off. Don't let negative thoughts overtake your dreams.

Too Much Sexual Intention

Many dream enthusiasts want to experience sexual fantasies as part of their lucid dream. It can be a great experience, but sometimes the intention is too strong. When you think about dream sex too much, the experience becomes overwhelming, and you have less control over your dream. This situation leads to your dream characters changing or waking up from excitement.

Myths About Lucid Dreaming

Lucid dreaming is an experience like no other and one that many people chase. In the process, some people start to make up their own ideas or get carried away with lucid dreaming myths. It can prevent you from proper lucid dreaming so let's set the record straight.

Myth: You Can Dream the Entire Night

Most people dream for about 90 to 100 minutes each night and mostly while experiencing REM sleep. Your first dream lasts about 10 minutes, while later dreams range in length from 20 to 45 minutes each.

Myth: Only Spiritual People Have Lucid Dreams

You do not have to be spiritual or religious to have lucid dreams. Anyone can lucid dream, and some people do it without trying, so it definitely does not have links to spirituality. Imagination and creativity allow a person to have lucid dreams along with the techniques explained in this book.

Myth: Others Can Share Your Lucid Dream

There is no way that someone else can share in your dream because it is unique to you. You might use input from someone else, like ideas for visualization, but others will not be able to enter your dream and share the experience with you.

Myth: Lucid Dreams Are Scary

Lucid dreams do not have to be scary because you control the narrative within the dream. However, a lucid dream might start off scary, like when you experience a nightmare, but once you become aware, you can change the direction of the dream. Some people decide to remain in the "scary" dream once they become conscious because it gives them an opportunity to explore their fears and understand them in a new way.

Myth: You Can Control the Whole Dream

Controlling every part of a lucid dream takes years of practice and a thorough understanding of how lucid dreams work. Beginners struggle to gain control in their lucid dreams and need to have frequent lucid dreams to strengthen their power while dreaming. Enjoy the experience of lucid dreaming rather than attempting to control everything.

Myth: Lucid Dreams Cause Mental Problems

Lucid dreaming cannot cause mental illness, but individuals with mental illness might find lucid dreaming alarming. Lucid dreaming is an interesting experience that lets you escape into another world so you can forget about your worries and wake up feeling refreshed.

Myth: Getting Stuck in Dreams Is Possible

You cannot get stuck in a dream because that is not how your sleep cycle works. Sometimes, dreams feel like they are continuing forever, but most likely, you have only been dreaming for approximately 20 minutes. Your dream will come to an end when your brainwaves change to a new pattern, such as when leaving or entering REM sleep.

Myth: Chronic Diseases Heal With Lucid Dreams

Lucid dreaming cannot heal chronic or other health conditions. You cannot dream of a cure and think it will be in effect once you wake up—that is not possible. However, lucid dreaming can help you to deal with emotional issues and improve your health in general.

Myth: Lucid Dreams Are Meaningless

Lucid dreaming provides meaning to your life. You can use the dream process to set your imagination free and live out fantasies. Some people find lucid dreams helpful to deal with fears and nightmares as they have some control over what is happening. Lucid dreaming improves your awareness and strengthens the connection between body and mind.

Lucid Dreaming Tips

With so many different ways to induce lucid dreaming, it only makes sense that there should be some great tips for lucid dreaming. Some of these tips are common sense but are things we don't always pay attention to. These tips will improve your sleep quality and allow you to have better lucid dreams.

Get Comfortable and Prepare

Comfort is necessary while preparing for lucid dreaming and while you sleep. You need a comfortable area to relax or meditate, so ensure you have a quiet space where you can concentrate on lucid dreaming. You want to focus on setting intentions, relaxation, and inducing dreams so you cannot have distractions in your room. Your bed and linen should be clean and comfortable so that you do not experience discomfort during the night as it could disrupt your sleep. Wearing clothing made from light, breathable fabric helps to be comfortable in bed too.

Set an Ambient Temperature

The temperature of the room should be comfortable to allow for better sleep. You are more likely to experience lucid dreaming in a slightly warmer room as your skin temperature changes while sleeping. Don't set the air conditioner to low as a cold room forces your body to adapt to temperature changes, which disrupts your sleep.

Improve Relaxation and Awareness

Meditating or doing relaxation exercises before going to bed will increase your awareness and get you ready to enter into conscious sleep. It helps to clear your mind entirely and sets the scene for lucid dreaming. You can also light incense or use essential oils for aromatherapy to promote relaxation. Incense should be lit early on to ensure it burns away before you fall asleep. You can put out any aromatherapy candles too. Good choices include lavender, frankincense, and rose.

Plan Consumption Before Bed

Food and beverages keep your body active for several hours after consumption. Eat your last meal several hours before going to bed so that your body doesn't wake you with digestive issues. Problems like heartburn will also be less if you do not eat food right before going to bed. Try to drink only water in the hours leading up to sleep, and remember that water can help in waking you up for some induction techniques.

Avoid Stimulants and Drugs

Alcohol, caffeine, and drugs should be avoided if you want to experience lucid dreams. It is okay to take them occasionally during the day but stop drinking or taking them several hours before heading to bed. Drugs and stimulants provide energy and change the chemicals in your body and brain, which prevents proper sleep and decreases your chances of lucid dreaming.

Switch Off Devices

Electronic devices disrupt sleep and prevent you from relaxing entirely. Switch off your phone or put it somewhere that it cannot bother you. It could help to put it on silent so that it does not make a sound or vibrate. Switch off any other digital devices like laptops or music players as well. You can put on some quiet music or lucid dreaming music to help you sleep if you find it helpful. Keep the lighting in your room to a minimum so that it does not disrupt you. If you do want some sort of light in your room, then opt for something with a blue hue as it promotes sleep.

Lucid dreaming is strongest when you develop excellent visualization skills and understand that your daily habits affect your chances of lucid dreaming. The WILD method is one of the most popular techniques for lucid dreaming but requires more practice and patience. Use the visualization strategies in this chapter to improve your skills for WILD, and remember that you can use them in any other method that requires visualization. To improve your lucid dreams, work on correcting your mistakes and forget about myths related to lucid, then try the tips that will boost your sleep quality and lucid dream experience.

Chapter 6:

You're in Control of Your

Dream

You have already taken the first steps towards lucid dreaming. You know how to induce lucid dreams, and how to use visualization and awareness strategies, and you have the ability to realize when you are dreaming. Now, the real fun starts! It is time to explore your lucid dreams fully, spend more time dreaming, and take control of aspects of your dream.

Staying Asleep

Beginner lucid dreamers frequently wake up as soon as they become lucid. Luckily, you can work on your lucidity skills and remain conscious for longer with some practice. The techniques in this section require you to perform an action in your dream, especially when your dream starts to fade so that you can remain in it for longer. The basic idea is that doing an action will load your perceptual system so that your concentration remains in the dream world instead of moving into the waking world.

Realize a Dream Is Ending

You need to realize when a dream is starting to end if you want to continue lucid dreaming. There are a few things that indicate the end of a dream is approaching. Usually, color is one of the first things that start to fade in a dream, followed soon after by some of the visual imagery disappearing from the landscape. The landscape can fade very quickly, so you need to recognize this issue as soon as possible. Once you realize the changes in the landscape, you need to take action to remain lucid.

How to Lucid Dream for Longer

The secret to remaining conscious in a lucid dream is being an active participant and paying attention. There are many ways to remain aware so try some of these strategies in your next lucid dream. After a while, you will find that these methods become critical to your lucid dreams and become so ingrained that you do them without much notice.

p.   Reality Check

By this time, you know that reality checks are very important in the waking and dream world. Do a reality check as soon as you realize you are dreaming or anytime the scene changes. Continue with reality checks through the dream and if the scene starts to fade. One of the easiest reality checks is to try and push your fingers straight through the palm of your other hand. Reality checks are a great tool to remain lucid even when your dream is stable.

q. *Spinning*

Spinning around and around is a useful action in lucid dreams. It helps to become aware in dreams, and many people use it as their transportation method through the dreamscape. It is effective to change your dreamscape entirely and allows you to get away from bad situations (like nightmares) very quickly.

Use your dream body to spin around on its axis. Concentrate on spinning even faster while the scene around you fades away. The fading indicates that you are ready to enter a new dream scene. Affirm to yourself, "I am in a dream," and believe it, then slow your spinning until your stop. Do a reality check as soon as the new dream landscape appears.

r. *Use Your Hands*

Take a moment to look at your hands in the waking world. They are quite essential and help with a lot of real-world activities. You also require your hands in the dream world so that you can do all kinds of things and experience the landscape through touch. Your hands form part of the lucid world, so use them to ground you, even if the rest of the dreamscape fades.

The first method you can use is to look at your hands in the dream world just like you would in the waking world. Concentrate fully on your hands so that you can increase the awareness of your entire body. Once your hands are in full focus, try looking up and become aware of the rest of the landscape.

The second method is a kinetic (movement) method. Rubbing your hands together draws your attention to the dream world instead of pulling it to the waking world. Look away from the scenery and at your hands. Start rubbing your hands together vigorously when the scene begins to fade. Continue to rub your hands together so that your dream body remains present and aware. Feel the friction and reaffirm that you will be in a dream when you look up.

s.   *Use Your Senses*

A multisensory experience is possible in any lucid dream and forms part of visualization techniques. Using all your senses is an ideal way to become more aware of your dream scene and stabilizes the landscape. Look around for the nearest object in your dream and set an intention to experience it with your sense. Pick up the object or touch it to provide tactile stimulation. Focus on how it feels, what it looks like, or use any other senses, like taste or hearing, to increase your awareness.

t. Ask for Clarity

You are in a dream, so you can do things that you cannot do in real life. You cannot ask life about its purpose, but you can do this in a lucid dream! In essence, you are asking your subconscious to recognize it is in a dream and provide clarity about what is happening in the dream. Start the process by selecting a key phrase, for example, "Increase the vividness of this dream," or "Increase my lucidity." Say your chosen mantra while lucid dreaming and believe what you ask for will happen. Maintain a positive attitude by phrasing your mantra with positive words instead of negativity. For example, say "I am dreaming" instead of "Don't wake up."

u. Look at the Ground

The ground beneath your feet serves as a reminder of your location—a dream! This stabilization method takes away any feelings of shakiness so that you can experience your dream fully. Once a dream starts to fade, look directly at the ground. Concentrate on the ground and how it feels beneath your feet so that you can improve your awareness. Look towards the horizon and at the rest of the landscape once you feel stable on the ground. Repeat this exercise until you see the dream in greater clarity.

v. *Shake Your Head*

Another kinetic technique is shaking your head when a dream starts fading. Begin by shaking your head slowly from side to side and then increase the speed. Repeat an affirmation that the next scene will be a dream, or demand clarity while shaking your head to improve the landscape around you or move to the next dream scene. Most people close their eyes when shaking their head, but this could cause you to wake up—it is something you will have to test while dreaming. If you do wake up, then try shaking your head with your eyes open to remain aware of the dream. Do a reality check if the scene changes and if you wake up because you might have a false awakening.

w. *Jump*

Jumping is another kinetic method similar to spinning and shaking your head. Jumping allows your dream body to feel the ground under your feet as you connect with it. Start by making small movements and move gradually. You can jump faster, but it causes some people to wake up. Try different speeds to find the best one for you. Hop a few times on the spot if you want the current landscape to become more vivid or take a larger leap with the intention to jump into a different scene.

x. Do Math

Math is an interesting way to improve your awareness. You can do any simple addition, subtraction, multiplication, or division to stimulate your consciousness. Someone with greater mathematics knowledge could try more complex calculations.

y. Relax

Relaxation is a necessary element to enter the lucid dream world, but you can use it to lengthen your dream as well. Many people lose their dream scene or wake up because they got too excited and it triggered their mind to return to the waking world. Slow down as soon as you realize you are in a dream, and take a moment to observe your surroundings. Immerse yourself in the landscape and stabilize the dream before you embark on crazy activities like flying.

z. Keep Going

Whenever you dream, you are doing an action, even if it is just to observe the scenery. This action requires awareness so you can use it to concentrate more on the dream world. Focus on going with the flow even if the scene fades away around you. Set your intention clearly by saying, "I will see a dream scene," while continuing with your activity. Do a reality check once a new landscape appears.

aa. Interact With the Dream Scene

Immersing yourself in the dreamscape makes you more aware of what is happening around you. The easiest way to immerse yourself is to use your senses: observe, listen, touch, taste, or smell different elements to make the dream more vivid. Move around the landscape so that you constantly have additional visual stimulation. You could also find a character within your dream; talk to them as it requires a lot more focus on lucidity.

bb. Fall Back

Falling backward might be a scary thought in real life, but it allows you to enter a new dreamscape as the current one fades away. Start by imagining your new dream scene and verbalize your intention. Fall straight back with the firm belief you will enter the new scene. This experience can be strange because it may feel as if you are falling physically. This sensation could cause you to wake up if your mind alerts your subconscious to this frightening experience. Try this technique with your eyes open and closed to find the one that works best.

cc. Supplements and Herbs

There are supplements and herbs available that improve your sleep quality and encourage REM cycles. The advantages of supplements are that the dream becomes more vivid, you gain better control, and awareness increases. Do some research about the supplements and herbs available in your area and determine the best one for you. Take them for several days or weeks to help your lucid dream efforts. Supplements and herbs won't help alone, so ensure you manage some of the other techniques.

dd. Use Language

Language is something a person uses from an early age—you learn to talk, think, and behave through communication. Your communication and language skills are some of your best tools to use in dreams. One way to prevent losing lucidity is to provide verbal directions or speak to yourself in your dream. Saying, "I am dreaming" is one of the fastest ways to remain lucid and acknowledge you are dreaming. Do it often while lucid dreaming so that you can prolong the experience.

Premature Awakening

Sometimes, you will wake up early and wish you could still continue dreaming. The best way to return to your dream is to play dead. Lie extremely still so that sleep paralysis can set in easily while your mind remains conscious. Remain motionless in bed and relax your body entirely or try one of the relaxation methods mentioned earlier. There is a great likelihood that your body will fall asleep again and allow you to enter a REM cycle, giving you the chance to lucid dream.

Awakening at Will

Waking up from a lucid dream when you want is really easy. All you need to do is to stop participating in the dream and pay it no attention. Withdrawing from the dream will reduce your awareness and let you wake up as soon as you want. There are various methods to wake up from a dream, and you might find that the dreamscape affects your choice of technique.

Call for Help

If you want to leave a dream, then you could call out for help. Your vocal cords aren't working due to sleep paralysis—calling for help in your dream might be a very quiet whisper. Close your eyes and focus on saying, "I need help." Repeat this request again and again while focusing on saying it louder until you wake up. You might utter the words in the real world, but it could just be a mental voice that alerts you to wake up.

Verbalize Your Intention

Sometimes, the easiest way to get out of a dream is to simply say, "Wake up!" You need to give this intention to your dream body and verbalize the request. Believe that you will wake up as you make the statement and ignore anything else happening in your dream.

Blink

Consciously opening and closing your eyes while dreaming focuses on you instead of the landscape, so the dream starts to fade away. As this happens, your brain refocuses on the waking world, and you find that you wake up after blinking in your dream. This technique brings you out of a lucid dream rapidly—you might still be experiencing sleep paralysis. Remain calm while your body wakes up and start doing reality checks to help you confirm your whereabouts.

Move Around

Sleep paralysis sets in when you are in a REM sleep cycle, so focusing on movement in the physical world can jolt you from your dream state. Withdraw from the dream by moving your arms and legs around as much as possible. Do not concentrate on the dream at all and just focus on your movements. It could help you to wake up, especially if you were sleeping in a comfortable position.

Fall Asleep

A great way to stop participating in a dream is to fall asleep (in the dream). It is not as easy as closing your eyes and falling asleep because there are other things happening in the landscape. Keep in mind that some characters might be talking or animals could be making noise. Ask everyone to be quiet to reduce distractions. Use your dream body to lie face down on the ground with your arms at your sides and close your eyes. It should help you to wake up in the real world soon enough.

Use Lighting

Lighting naturally wakes a person from their sleep or at least makes them light sleepers. It could help you to wake up more easily from your dreams. Blue lighting stimulates sleep and dreaming, so choose a different color lighting to wake you up. This method could weaken your sleep quality and cause sleep deprivation if you don't get sufficient quality sleep.

Use an Alarm

Any alarm will wake you up from sleep. You can set an alarm to ring in about 90 minutes since that is roughly when REM sleep repeats. You will wake up once the alarm rings but ensure you have to switch it off properly so that you do not remain asleep. This method will wake you up, but it is not ideal because you need REM sleep for proper brain and body functioning. Interrupting your sleep frequently can cause sleep deprivation, so only use this method if you really need to.

Controlling Your Dreams

The aim of most lucid dreamers is to create and control their own dream scenes. It is exhilarating to do whatever you want in your dream and gives you a sense of control even when it feels like your real life is out of control. You need to try various strategies within your dreams to see what works best for you. Once you find your go-to strategies, you can practice using them in your dreams and control the dream narrative.

Setting Goals

Try controlling your dreams by setting intentions or dream goals while you are awake. Spend some time daydreaming or visualizing your entire dream narrative or a specific activity. Add all your senses to the dream and focus on your role in the dream. Imagine how you are going to achieve your goal and rehearse it in your mind until you can do it without much thought. Repeat the process as many times as necessary until you feel you can do it in your dreams without a second thought. Once you are ready, set a dream intention and use an induction method to achieve lucid dreaming, then try out your goal just like you practiced in the waking world.

Stabilization

Stabilization is any method you use to bring greater awareness to your dreams and to remain lucid. You can use stabilization or grounding techniques to control your dreams because they are mainly found in control. Use visualization to create the object or scene you want in your dream and focus on all its features to gain greater control. If things aren't going according to plan, then concentrate on your breathing for a few moments to slow down before refocusing on the dream object or scene.

Verbalization

Verbalization requires speaking your wants to dream characters, objects, or your subconscious. Once you decide to do something in your dream, verbalize it and believe it will happen. For example, approach a dream character and ask, "Will you guide me through the forest?" or talk to your subconscious by asking the scene to freeze or stating another demand. You truly need to believe that what you ask will materialize; there is no space for doubt.

Use an Object

Dream objects are anything that can be found in your dream. Some people find that dream objects, like a door or portal, allow them to move to a new dreamscape.

Others find a dream object to help them gain control, such as finding a magic wand that changes things to your heart's desire, almost like how Alice consumed different things to move through Wonderland.

Manage Emotions

Some dreams have negative aspects, bad characters, or become full-blown nightmares. Your attitude towards these elements could become negative if you don't remain aware. Make a conscious choice to control these things by using positive emotions. You could hug a sad character, rescue a hurt animal, or simply send positive thoughts towards the landscape. Some people find that using positive emotions can help to confront nightmares and overcome fears.

Use Your Body

Your dream body can do all kinds of things in your dream world so try all kinds of things while lucid. A popular technique is to start running or taking leaps, which leads to flight. Other people flap their arms up and down like a bird and realize they are starting to lift off the ground in flight. You might find that you can wrap yourself into a ball and roll right into a new dream scene. The only limitation is your mind, so set a dream intention and visualize these things happening in the waking world so that you can experience it in the dream world.

Use Insights

Sometimes, you set a goal for a dream, but you keep getting other prompts while being lucid. These prompts are insights and could be underlying thoughts, a fear, anxiety, or something else that recently happened and requires attention. Use these insights to control your dreams by letting go of your original plan and following the prompts to create a new dream plot. You can still control the dream since you are only using the insights as an inspiration. It might be a good idea to ask your subconscious what it wants to show you or to demand clarity so that you can continue with the dream.

Passive Observation

There are times when you simply cannot control your dream event though you are lucid. You have already done reality checks, stabilized the dream, and tried every grounding technique possible but without any success—you still cannot do what you want in the dreamscape. No matter how hard you try, you remain a spectator watching from the edge of the dream, or you might feel like you are floating in the air and looking down at the landscape. Realize that you do not always have to control your dream. Sometimes, the best method of control is to let it go and just enjoy what is playing out in front of your eyes. Being a passive observer can be an enjoyable and calming experience. A huge benefit of observation is that you can see everything in your dream and use it to strengthen your dream recall for your next visit to this dream scene.

Maintaining Dream Control

Dream control is a fascinating concept, but it doesn't always work. Sometimes you cannot control a specific aspect, which can be frustrating, but it is not a big deal. There are times when you should simply go with the flow and allow yourself to be a passive observer in the dreamscape. Alternatively, the lack of control could be due to improper lucid dreaming strategies.

- The first problem with control occurs if you did not stabilize your dream. Do a reality check immediately once you become aware of the dream and say, "I'm dreaming."
- Another issue is poor reality checking. You need to repeat grounding exercises and reality checks frequently during your dream to remain lucid.
- A big problem is forgetting to set an intention for your dream. Always set an intention; otherwise, you have no idea of what is happening in your dream.

Not having control is not a huge problem. Your dream might not be what you anticipated, but you could still have a fulfilling experience. Be an observer and take in all of the landscape so that you can recall it properly.

Write down all the details in your dream journal so that you can return to the dreamscape at a later time with clear intentions.

Manipulating the Content of Your Dream

Manipulation and control are similar aspects and can be used together to dictate your dream narrative. Manipulation usually occurs when you want to achieve something specific, and you have to set goals before you attempt these tactics. Usually, a person practices one technique several times until you become a master and use it in your dream without much effort.

How to Fly

Flying is a common dream goal for most people and a great way to travel through the landscape or a new dream scene entirely. Flying is not something you can do in real life, although you can do it in your dream. However, realities and uncertainties from the waking world frequently find their way into dreams, so you might find that you become scared of falling once you start flying, especially as you go higher.

The way you start flying is up to you entirely. Some people verbalize their desire and start flying immediately, while others complete a kinetic action to get some momentum. Start by setting the intention to fly and use a visualization strategy when you are awake to rehearse your actions. Once you enter the dream world, try taking big jumps forward several times or run as fast as you can until your feet leave the ground. You might find that falling forward off a ledge allows flying to set in. If you really want, try the superhero technique and simply put one arm up in the air to activate your flying abilities.

Whichever method you choose, remember to practice it for several weeks so that you can increase your confidence. Flying might not come naturally, but even small accomplishments, such as jumping higher, shows progress, so keep going. If you are struggling to fly, then consider using a flying aid in your dreams to boost your abilities. You could morph yourself into a butterfly so that you have wings or add a jetpack to achieve liftoff. If nothing seems to work, then get another dream object to fly for you, like having a private jet on standby or clicking your fingers for a large bird to appear, then ride on its back. The possibilities are endless, and no idea is too bizarre, so go wild!

Change the Scenery

Changing the landscape and objects in it is not as easy as visualizing it to be that way. Usually, you want to change the scenery because you want something different from the dream than you previously intended. Perhaps you see an element you don't like and want to change it. To change the scenery, you must believe that it will change and set an intention as well as finding a way to change it. You can find a dream object, like a door, that will open up to a new landscape once you walk through it. Alternatively, look straight in front of you and verbalize your intended dream scene, then turn around and believe your new scene will appear. The most important thing is to have faith in the change and then find a way to effect change.

Travel Through Time

Traveling through time is one of the easiest things you can do in lucid dreams. All you need to do is find the best way to time travel. A really good way to time travel is to fly high into the air until you only see clouds, visualize the time period you want, then return to the landscape into your desired place. Another method is to find an escalator and go up to move forward in time or take the escalator down and back into a previous time. You could also use a time machine to take you where you want. The most important thing with these methods is that you must visualize your chosen time and destination for a successful arrival. Time travel techniques also work to change the scenery. Consider combining these methods for an added thrill.

Find Dream Objects

Everything in the dreamscape is a dream object, but you might want to find one object specifically. Visualize the object you want, and then go about the dreamscape to find it since it won't simply appear before your eyes. The best way to find an object is to search for it in a sensible place. For example, you could visualize a mermaid that will lead you to an underwater world by looking for the mermaid in the ocean, or you might find your trusted pocket watch for time traveling by searching through a jewelry box.

Talk to Your Subconscious

Your subconscious helps to control your dreams and allows you to become lucid. Speaking to your subconscious allows you to verbalize your desires, even the crazy ones, in your dreams and can create a dream scene or object in front of your eyes. Once you become aware, speak out loud to your subconscious and see if you can find a response. In most cases, this is a bit of a stretch, and few people will "hear" anything back because they don't believe a response will happen. It is a much better method to create a dream character that represents your subconscious. You can then speak to the dream character and use them as a guide throughout the dream.

Create Dream Characters

Dream characters are any "living" things in your dream. It could be a person, an animal, or even a mythical creature. You might want to spend time walking with lions or meet a celebrity. The major problem with dream characters is that people get over-excited and wake up as soon as the character appears. You should remain calm throughout the process.

Around the Corner

A great way to meet a dream character is to visualize them being around the corner. Set an intention to see the character and verbalize your wishes, then walk around the corner and expect to walk into them. Call out to the character as soon as you go around the corner and allow their image to come into focus.

Ask the Dreamer

This method requires speaking to your subconscious or the person behind the dream to allow you to see a dream character. In its most basic form, all you need to do is to verbalize your wish, and it becomes an auto-suggestion that takes shape in your dream. If this all seems a little weird, then turn your subconscious into a dream character and make the request directly to your subconscious image.

Open a Door or Reach Through a Surface

Any type of dream portal can allow you to create dream characters. Start by visualizing your dream character, then find a way to get them into a dream by reaching out to them. You could open a door, stretch out your hand, and feel your dream character grasping your hand as you pull them through the door. Use the same strategies to reach into the water, through a mirror, or any other surface and pull your character into your dream. It is essential to visualize the character properly; otherwise, you might pull a total stranger into your dream.

Draw

Visualize the character you want in your dream, then use your hands to sketch their outline in the air. Don't worry if it is a crude drawing since the power lies in the visualization process. As you create the outline, the character will take shape and pop into the scene.

Photoshop

Photoshop and even mobile phone cameras can change an image in any way you wish. In most cases, your dream characters are not true to all their features because they are some type of composite. Once you visualize your dream character, ask your dream to make specific changes to the character so that it fits your desires. Verbalize your requests for change and do some action like waving your hand, snapping your fingers, or pressing a button to improve your dream character.

Shape-Shifting

Find something in your dreamscape that you can change into your dream character and verbalize your request for the object to change. The object doesn't have to look like your dream character at all because you are using the power of visualization to manipulate the object. For example, you could demand a log to become your dream character. Use the power of will to realize your dream character.

Lucid Dream Incubation

Dream incubation brings all the strategies for lucid dreaming together. You can compare lucid dream incubation to planting a seed. Plants require time to grow and frequent attention to reach their full potential. This same strategy applies to lucid dreaming too. You have to work on it frequently and allow it time to strengthen.

Create

The first step to lucid dream control is to set an intention for your dream. Consider the intention to be the seed that you plant, such as flying, meeting a new character, or visiting a different landscape. Your intention should consist of a single idea.

Reaffirm

Reaffirm your dream intention by creating a mantra that allows you to plant the seed inside your mind. Use clear words to emphasize your affirmation, such as "I will fly in my next dream," or "I will find a time travel device in my next dream." Repeat this affirmation as many times as possible and refocus your attention if your mind wanders.

Visualize

Visualization is crucial if you want your intention to succeed. Spend sufficient time to think about your dream contents and sketch it out in your mind. This landscape is the soil that covers your intention and supports it in growth. For example, you need an open sky to fly through the air.

Repeat

Repeat your mantra and visualize often to strengthen the thought in your mind. Repetition is a watering exercise that allows your dream intention to stabilize as it becomes part of your life. This repetition encourages the belief that a dream will happen.

Release

Let go of your dream intention and visualization once you start falling asleep. Give the idea to your subconscious and believe that it will appear throughout the night.

Recall

Recall your dreams once you wake up. Write down all your dreams from the night in great detail and determine whether your dream intention became true. Concentrate on whether the intention appeared at all and how it is progressing as you visualize it more until you manage to fulfill the intention completely.

Overcoming a Lucid Dream Dry Spell

All of us want to experience lucid dreaming, but sometimes, lucidity eludes us, and we go weeks or months without a single lucid dream. It is frustrating, especially if you are working hard at learning techniques and not getting any results. The strange thing about lucidity is that it becomes elusive if we want it too much. So, take a step back and consider what might be causing your lucid dreaming dry spell.

Beginner Issues

Novice lucid dreamers might wait months before they experience lucidity. In reality, this is not a dry spell because you haven't experienced continuous lucidity previously, but it is still a frustrating feeling. Beginner lucid dreamers must make a conscious effort to advance their skills. Start with the basics in the beginning chapters of this book and ensure you mastered the techniques.

Practice reality checks, relaxation strategies, visualization, and dream recall so that you can strengthen your lucid dreaming foundation and then move on to induction techniques. Look through the potential mistakes section, too, so that you are sure you are doing everything correctly. Be patient with yourself and believe in your lucid dreaming abilities. It will pay off eventually.

Sleep Deprivation

Insufficient or poor-quality sleep is a major problem for lucid dreamers. Sometimes, life is busy, and you get less sleep or don't go through enough REM cycles to dream. Jet lag, stress, or health concerns can suppress your sleep too, which decreases your chances of lucidity. The basic solution to this problem is to sleep more without distractions. This is easier said than done, especially if you cannot make constructive changes to the underlying problem causing your sleep deprivation.

If you cannot address the sleep deprivation, then accept that lucid dreaming is not possible and try again once you get more sleep. You could try to sleep just an hour more each night as it might encourage your REM sleep cycles. Try breaking your sleep into blocks of two to four hours and sleep a few times during the day or night like parents would with a newborn baby.

Insufficient Self-Awareness

This lucid dreaming problem has its origins in the waking world. You need proper self-awareness while awake if you want to achieve lucidity at night. Focus on doing reality checks while awake and practice awareness exercises like those in Chapter 1 to improve your awareness.

Incubation

Many people expect to have a lucid dream once they get in bed but haven't thought about lucid dreaming all day. They do not practice dream incubation and don't use any awareness strategies such as journaling or recall. You don't have to spend a lot of time on lucid dreaming; just give it about 15 minutes a day where you start setting intentions for lucidity and concentrate on dream recall.

Lucid dreaming opens the door to a fascinating world where anything is possible. Being able to control your dreams allows you to create your own narrative and improves your imagination. There are tons of options for lucid dreams, so try some of the strategies in this chapter to encourage your lucid dream abilities.

Chapter 7:

It's Time to Explore and Be Amazed

What would you like to do with your improved lucid dreaming skills? Take a few moments to jot down some ideas and think entirely out of the box. Make a sort of wish list in your dream journal and fill it with some cool ideas. In this chapter, we will look at a whole lot of things you can do while lucid dreaming, including sexual dreams. Use these prompts as inspiration for your lucid dreams and try some of these techniques for a greater experience. Remember to follow the steps you learned previously correctly so that you can have an optimal experience.

Challenges for Beginners

Flying is probably one of the first things lucid dreamers want to do, but there are so many other options. These first few ideas are perfect challenges for novice lucid dreamers. These challenges will help you focus on dream intentions with little complexity while having a fun experience. Experiment with creating dream objects, finding supernatural skills, and improving your sensory experiences.

Consume Your Favorites

All of us have a favorite food, drink, dessert, or another treat. You can probably visualize it right now, so you should have no problem visualizing it in your dream. Start by setting the intention to eat your favorites in your dream and visualize the restaurant or edible before you go to bed. Once in your dream, find the restaurant or shop where you can get it. Alternatively, draw it in the air or on a flat surface and watch as it comes to life in front of your eyes. You can now enjoy your item! Spend a few moments to smell it and then taste the product. It will be just as amazing as in real life. The best part is that this is a dream. Have as many as you want since everything is calorie-free!

Move Through a Wall

Some people may have punched a wall and took out a piece of it in the waking world, but the lucid world is so much better because you can move right through walls and other solid surfaces. Moving through walls allows you to travel from one place to another quickly and might change the dream scene as well. It is also a reality check because this is not something you can do in real life, so it immediately enhances your awareness.

Start by finding a wall in your dream. Visualize your hand and body moving through it and consider it to be an object through which you can move. Do not consider it to be solid. Once you are at the wall, push your hand gently towards and through the wall while expecting it to move right through. It might help to visualize yourself as a ghost since we expect ghosts to move through solid surfaces. Another method is to run directly at a wall with the full knowledge that you are going to pass through it. Some people find that moving slowly causes them to hit their face and bounce back from the wall due to hesitation or disbelief.

Be an Amazed Observer

Every one of us wants to control a dream, but novice dreamers can learn a lot from observation. It is always an option to give up control and take time to look at what is going on around you. Find a suitable observation point in the landscape and move to that place. A skyscraper, lookout point, or the edge of the landscape make great observation points. Once you reach this place, look across the landscape at everything that is happening in your dream and find all the small details. Your increased awareness through observation (using all your senses) will help with dream recall, and you can plan for what you want to do the next time you visit this scene.

Another observation method is to move through the landscape without controlling it. Use your time to look at things in more detail, explore the terrain, notice smells and sounds, or interact with dream objects. You could also strike up a conversation with a dream character but without steering the conversation in a specific direction. If you find you want to start controlling the dream, then ask your dream to show you something amazing and wait for a plot twist.

Be Surprised by a Dream Character

Dream characters will appear from your visualizations or be a part of the dream scene automatically. They can be a source of interest to you and provide a lot of information. Ask a dream character to show you around the landscape to increase your awareness. You could even ask them to take you to a secret place or the most exciting area in your dream. For a truly surprising result, ask your dream character to tell you a joke. This is quite fun since you are essentially asking your subconscious to tell you a joke, but the results will leave you in awe.

Turn Day Into Night

Changing a dream scene might seem a bit daunting for beginners, so a good starting point is to change day into night. Look at the clear sky, then to the ground and visualize the night sky, then look back to the sky and expect it to be nighttime. Another method is to use your hand as a paintbrush and move across the sky in broad strokes to change the color. Some people use their breath and blow darkness into the air for a change. Enjoy this visual treat and the star-flecked sky. Now is a great time to try out your flying skills or play dot-to-dot with the popular star signs to turn them into drawings.

Be a Magician

If the idea of dream control seems a bit far-fetched to you, then maybe you should try becoming a dream character that could have control, like a magician. Once you become a magician, try to pull a rabbit out of a hat, concoct a magic spell, or use your magic wand to change things in your dream.

Do a Good Deed

Use your lucid dream to spread some good cheer to your dream characters and surroundings. This is a great beginner activity because you can do these things quite easily. Find something or someone in your dream and help them out. It could be to save a turtle from trash caught around its body, buy a dream character a meal, or help to build a house. The possibilities are endless, and you will wake up with a sense of goodwill that you can take with you throughout your waking day.

Find a Philosopher

Dream characters have different personalities, interests, and abilities so make use of the source of knowledge at your fingertips. Connect with a philosopher in your dream by asking another character where to find one or visualize a philosopher and have them come to life. Now, ask the philosopher all kinds of existential questions. Ask about the meaning of life, who you really are, and what the future holds. These types of questions allow you to have a two-way conversation with your subconscious and may identify your greatest desires or fears.

Intermediate Challenges

The next set of challenges require more awareness and a good sense of dream control. These challenges consider things that are of interest in the real world, and many people still don't have the answers to some of these questions, which makes these ideas fascinating.

Meet an Alternate Self

Some people believe that parallel universes exist along with ours, so you can explore this idea in your lucid dream and meet yourself. The idea behind a parallel universe is that it occurs every time you make a decision. For example, you might have chosen to go to college but there is a parallel universe in which your life plays out without going to college. This phenomenon is called the butterfly effect and can be a bit distressing if things did not happen according to your plan. However, meeting another version of yourself can be fascinating. Ask the dream to take you to meet yourself in a parallel universe but do not control any other elements of the dream. Simply go with the flow and experience the other person's life.

Attempt Thought Control

Dream characters are figments of your imagination, but they still have thoughts and feelings (created by your subconscious). Have a look around the scene and find a dream character that you want to know more about. Concentrate on this character and try to read their thoughts without controlling their thinking.

Use Quantum Physics

Quantum physics is the study of how things interact at an infinitesimal number. It requires extremely large or small proportions and scientists constantly want to discover more at these limits. The universe is so big that we cannot imagine it at full size, but your lucid dreaming can help you experience things from different perspectives. Once you are in a lucid dream, ask it to make your body 1,000 times smaller and observe the landscape from this vantage point. Everything could seem huge, but you might find interesting insight at this size, like studying the composition of a grain of sand. You could even ask to be shrunk another 1,000 times smaller and experience the dream world as a tiny human being. Add in some extra fun by trying out your flying or teleporting skills at this new size.

Travel to the Edge

Have you ever wondered about the edge of the universe or what is up there in the sky past your line of sight? You could find some answers to this question (even though they are made up by your subconscious) by exploring the edge of the universe in your lucid dream. Ask the dreamer to increase your size by 1,000 and have a look at the landscape from this greater size. Spend some time observing everything, then increase your body by another factor of 1,000. At this stage, you might be able to see a new universe or touch other planets in the solar system. Concentrate on your surroundings and the events as they unfold. Some people find thoughts or ideas floating around and relate this back to forgotten memories or underlying concerns.

Drive a Fast Car

There are so many luxury and fast cars on the market that you probably want to drive. Use your lucid dreams to drive as many different fast cars as you want. You can choose from current models or antique racing cars, or create your own brand of vehicle. Drive at breathtaking speeds without any fear.

Explore an Underwater World

Dive deep into the ocean, plummet into a waterfall, or explore underwater caves while lucid dreaming. You don't need any scuba diving gear because you have control in this world, so you can breathe comfortably underwater like a fish. Explore the water and all its glorious contents at depths unknown to man. You could even go visit the Titanic, find an underwater treasure trove, or find new marine species.

Find a Dream Pill

Before you try this challenge, do several reality checks to ensure you are dreaming. Search the dream scene for a mystery object, specifically, a pill. You might have to summon a drug dealer or find a chemist to give you one. Take this mystery pill and see where it takes you. Don't control the narrative; just go with the flow.

Advanced Challenges

Advanced challenges are an opportunity to test out all your lucid dream techniques and strategies. These challenges push your lucidity to the limit and require a great sense of awareness.

Speak a Different Language

Visit a new country in your dreams and communicate with the locals in their language. Speaking a foreign language while dreaming can be exhilarating, especially if you cannot speak it in real life. Ask the locals to show you the best places in the area and explore their culture with them. It could be an eye-opening experience and teach you things that you can use in the waking world, such as an openness to diversity or compassion.

Explore a New Planet

Take a lucid dreaming trip to a new planet of your liking. You can use mainstream ideas of planets where the aliens have strange features and travel in UFOs, or set up your entire planet according to your ideas. Start by visualizing the shape of the planet and its features. Determine its weather, what the inhabitants look like, or the different activities you can do. Find a citizen of this planet and strike up a conversation, like asking if they can show you around. Question them about moving to this planet.

Confuse a Dream Character

Approach a dream character and tell them that they are in a dream, then watch their reactions. The character might be puzzled, struggle to understand, disappear, or do something unpredictable. Don't control the character; rather, observe their actions as they realize they are imaginary.

The Void

A void is an open space without anything in it. In lucid dreaming, the void occurs when you let the dreamscape fade away in favor of open space so that the only thing left is you. This practice is closely related to Tibetan dream yoga and increases your awareness of yourself. It requires quietness within your mind and relinquishing control. Entering the void does not mean you are withdrawing your participation in the dream; it is the opposite. You are participating to such an extent that nothing exists. Simply observe the void and become aware of the space you take up in it. Let go of any other thoughts to remain in the void. Shapes and colors similar to hypnagogia may enter the void at times, but you can welcome these and observe them as they pass through time and space.

Control Weather and Nature

The weather is one of the things that none of us can control, but you can do it in the lucid world. Use your lucid dream power to change the weather as you wish. Try to do more than what would occur in the waking world. You can start off by standing under the clouds as a thunderstorm drenches your clothes or try a new perspective by experiencing the lightning show from above the clouds. You could even control the lightning to strike you for an extra thrill.

Imagine some natural disasters but control other elements like having a tornado rip through the landscape but leaving everything unharmed or seeing the earth rip open after an earthquake but giving way to a magnificent waterfall. You could run from an erupting volcano or use a tsunami to change your dream scene.

Explore the World of Mirrors

Create a dream scene where an entire room consists of mirrors and then have a good look at yourself. Pay attention to every detail of your character and see if you can identify things that are different to the waking world or determine if there is some aspect you could use for reality checking in the future, like finding you have a tail. You can also use the mirrors as portals to other dream scenes, so attempt to enter a scene representing your subconscious, a dark side, or a parallel universe.

Make Some Music

Most of us have a favorite song, play an instrument, or listen to music almost constantly throughout the day. Some people even fall asleep to music, so it obviously plays a big role in our lives. You can add music to your dreams by asking for a song to be played or activating a music button. It is your dream—you could even use an old jukebox.

Take the music one step further by making it yourself, even if you have never played an instrument before. Start by choosing an instrument and then commence playing. It doesn't even have to be a real instrument! You could be playing an air guitar and hear the sounds blasting through the atmosphere or be beating out a tune on some clouds instead of drums.

Making music is an amazing experience since you are using talents, but it is difficult to replicate the music in the waking world. If you find yourself making music in your dreams, then it might be time to start playing an instrument in real life. The main reason for being musical in the waking and dream world is that you can remember the music you made while dreaming more easily and reproduce it in real life. Several musicians have written songs or instrumental pieces after receiving a boost of inspiration through lucid dreaming.

Amazing Things to Do in a Dream

Lucid dreams are imaginary worlds that you can fill with your wildest desires. There are no limits in the dream world—get out of your comfort zone and do all the things that might seem impossible in the waking world.

A Fine Dining Experience

There are so many cooking shows these days that you might find yourself craving a seat at some of the elite establishments across the world. Book a seat at your preferred fine dining restaurant in your lucid dream for a culinary experience like no other. Remember to use all your senses during your dream to heighten the experience. It is also a great opportunity to try foods from different parts of the world or to be served by your favorite chef.

Meet Your Hero

Who is the one person you have always wanted to meet? Think of any person across time, continents, and other dimensions. Make a list of these people and use it to visualize them in your dreams so that you can meet them. It could be a famous sports star, a celebrity, an influential leader, or a historical figure. You can meet anyone! As an idea to start you off, go meet the Wright brothers and join them on their quest to develop and fly the first motor-operated plane.

Become a Zombie

Most people think about surviving a zombie invasion, and that is a lucid dream idea you might like to attempt. A way more interesting strategy is to become a zombie in your dream and see things from the other side. Go on an invasion mission and see if you can survive as a zombie being hunted by humans.

Go on a Date

The dream world is a great place to go on dates with real or imaginary people. Paint a dream world where you and your crush can go for a romantic date without the limitations of the real world. Travel with them through different scenes, do interesting activities, or let your date take control of your dreams and ask them to show you something amazing.

Generate More Limbs

The waking life can be so busy that you might feel you need more hands or another head to get everything done, so why not try this in your dreams? Once you become lucid, change yourself to have more limbs, an extra head, supersonic hearing, or an extra eye. Use these limbs to do things at lightning speed or go for a walk in the dreamscape and see how other dream characters react to your modifications.

Be a Movie Star

Construct a dream scene consisting of a movie set filled with all the necessary props, actors, and other film crew. Be a movie star in your own film and see what it is like. This is a lucid dream prompt that you can use over and over again. Try playing the main role, a supporting role, being the hero, and the villain. You could also use movies from different genres. Set the scene for action, a romantic encounter, or change everyone into animation film characters.

Choose Lottery Numbers

Create a dream scene to produce a lottery machine or visualize a television program that reads out the lottery numbers. You could also set an intention to find lottery numbers in the dreamscape and then search the entire scene for numbers, such as in dream advertisements, in the sand, or by asking dream characters for a number. Take note of these numbers and use them to play the lottery in real life. This challenge will test your dream recall abilities quite well. You might win a few bucks, or it could be a bust, but it is something fun to try while dreaming.

Be a Rock Star

Become a rock star in your favorite band, take on the role of a popular music artist, or start your own act in the world of music. Imagine yourself decked out with the coolest clothes and create a unique artistic persona that entertains scores of people. Go on a world tour to meet your fans and play in festivals. Use this time to interact with your dream characters, take requests from doting fans, and experience the party lifestyle.

Spend Time With Animals

Create an entire landscape filled with some of the most exotic and dangerous animals available in the world and experience them from the safety of your dream. Take a ride on the back of a cheetah to experience their lightning speed, swim with sharks, or have a black mamba curl around your body. If you want a more gentle experience, then that is fine too. Try being in a ball pit full of cuddly puppies or rolling string with kittens. You could even ask the animals some poignant questions or try to learn their language. The amazing part about using animals in your lucid dreams is that they won't be harmed, and you can encounter them safely, which can be a wonderful thing if you are scared of them or have allergies in real life.

Explosions

Lucid dreams can help you release anger from the waking world. A great way to deal with anger is to make things explode in your dream. Start by planting explosives beneath boxes or in a junkyard and then press a magic button to make it explode. Another method is to point an imaginary gun at an object and pull the trigger, then watch as the object goes up in smoke.

Helpful Lucid Dreams

Lucid dreams are the ideal platform to prepare for all kinds of events. You can learn a new skill, improve your abilities, or rehearse nerve-wracking situations to ease the butterflies in your stomach. Here are some ways to use lucid dreams as preparation for events in the waking world.

Practice Your Hobby

The old adage is that practice makes perfect, but the waking world doesn't always afford us the opportunity to practice. There are financial constraints, too little time, and a hundred other things that might hold you back. Use your lucid dreams to practice the sport or hobby that you love. Hit a thousand cricket balls until you get the stroke just right, or build a new treehouse the size of a mansion. Do what you love without any of your real-world worries.

Revisit a Memory

Everyone has memories from the waking world that they hold dear to their heart. You can probably think of one already, and many people wish they could relive these memories. Use your lucid dreams to create a dreamscape that is similar to your memory and immerse yourself in the experience again. Take this opportunity to focus on the small details that you may have missed the first time around.

Job Interviews

No one knows what to expect from a job interview, but you always want to put your best foot forward. Set an intention to attend a job interview in your dream and use this opportunity to answer all kinds of interview questions. Recall your dream in the morning to identify strengths or weaknesses and any questions that require more thorough or thoughtful answers. Next time, try the interview process from the other side of the desk so that you are the person asking the questions of a potential job candidate. It might give you another perspective of what potential employers want from their interviews.

Walk in Someone Else's Shoes

Sometimes you might wonder what exactly is going on in another person's mind or maybe you don't understand a person but really want to. Decide to take on this person's character in your lucid dream and experience life from their perspective. This is an exercise in empathy, and you might find a lot of insights about the other person that you did not consider previously. Use these insights as inspiration in the waking world to be more compassionate towards others.

Say Goodbye

Lucid dreams provide an opportunity to see a deceased loved one. Meet your loved one in a favorite spot and experience some time with them before saying goodbye a final time. Use this opportunity to say everything to them that you didn't get the chance to say in the waking world and hold them tight one last time before releasing them to the light.

Explore Your Life

Lucid dreams provide mental clarity when you are uncertain about things in your waking life. You can ask the lucid dream to show you what it (you) wants out of life or find answers to life-altering questions. It could be useful to use your subconscious as a dream character and ask your subconscious to shed light on the important things in your life. Visualize your life as you want it to be in the future and find clarity about your goals.

A Guardian Angel

If you feel insecure, then one of the best things you could do is to understand that you are protected in the dream world and when awake. Ask the dream to show you your guardian angel or use dream character techniques to create one. Meet your guardian angel and tell them your concerns, then ask for them to protect you.

Find a Mentor

Visualize a mentor to meet in your dreams or ask your dream characters to point you to a mentor. The person could be an influential historical figure, a prominent businessman, or a college coach. Ask the mentor to guide you in becoming a better person and tell them you want to learn from them. Try asking the questions, "What should I know?" or "What is the most important thing you can teach me?" to start the conversation. Use these learnings in your waking life to become a better person.

Explore Technology

Futuristic technologies are attractive to many people, and lucid dreaming gives you an opportunity to explore technology in the ways you want. Create a dreamscape consisting of futuristic elements or use futuristic technology to interact in your dream.

Travel Into Space

Space, the moon, planets, and hidden galaxies are something that many people want to see and experience. But, you can only do this in the real world if you are an astronaut or if you can fork out a couple hundred thousand dollars for a trip from SpaceX or Virgin Galactic, and these services are still in a testing phase. Your lucid dream can be the ideal time to travel into space and explore it in all kinds of ways. Instead of using your usual lucid dream time-traveling skills, opt for a futuristic method of travel. Board the Virgin Galactic or SpaceX rocket for a luxury trip into space and enjoy all the millionaire amenities along the way.

Use Augmented Reality

Augmented reality is something that already exists in the real world. It is the ability to use digital technologies to provide information that you wouldn't otherwise know. Think about it like putting on technologically-driven glasses that provide the name, birth date, and interests of any person you look at while wearing these glasses. Another method is to aim your phone or another digital device at an area, like houses, for more information on its occupants or other insights. Find an augmented reality device in your lucid dream and use it to explore your surroundings while getting unique information. Let the dream control what information is given for an added thrill.

Travel on the Hyperloop

Elon Musk is one of the most futuristic idealists of all time, and he has a conceptual transport method called the Hyperloop. It is a high-speed bullet-type idea with exciting prospects. The transportation device is a pressurized capsule found in a steel tube with reduced pressure situated 20-feet above ground. The capsule rides on air using air compressors and induction motors. According to Musk, the Hyperloop will travel at speeds in excess of 760 mph. Summon the Hyperloop in your lucid dream and travel at crazy speeds from one dream scene to the next.

Try 4D Printing

3D printing is something that many people are trying out in the waking world, but it can be quite expensive. Now, scientists and technicians are considering adding another dimension to this process—time. With 4D printing, you can print anything you want in any time period you want. Create a 4D printing machine in your lucid dream and use it to print your ideal dream scene in a specific period, then explore this new world. Try printing a space station on Venus so that you can explore the planet, or maybe you want some bionic limbs to take part in an intergalactic war.

Visit Project Utopia

Project Utopia is a dream yacht island from Russian oligarchs. This is the ideal holiday destination if you are ready to move on from a lucid dream superyacht experience. Project Utopia is a type of private cruise liner in the middle of the ocean, which consists of several stories, a panoramic observation deck, a shopping area, entertainment theaters, a range of food outlets, fancy restaurants, pools, and anything else your heart desires. Visit Project Utopia in your lucid dreams for a luxury holiday experience. This destination has so many things to do that you might want to explore it over several dreams.

Moment Everyone's Been Waiting for: Dream Sex

Sexual dreams are some of the best ones you can experience, but they require patience, practice, and a calm state of mind. You can create any sex scene while lucid dreaming because it is an imaginary world of your creation. It is a safe space to explore your sexual desires without fear of repercussion or worldly norms, even if this idea does seem a bit strange.

Dream sex can feel very real because of your heightened awareness. During REM sleep, your body experiences fluctuations in arousal, and this may trigger your subconscious while lucid dreaming, even if you didn't set a sexual intention. Dream orgasms can manifest in your physical body, and you may experience muscle responses as a result. There is also a lot of speculation that wet dreams (ejaculating while asleep) could occur due to sexual encounters in dreams, whether lucid or non-lucid.

You can set a lucid dream intention with lots of visualization for a sexual encounter or simply find a dream character once lucid and decide to have a sexual experience. Sometimes it happens naturally in a dream, and this is an ideal time to go with the flow. The most important thing to remember during sexual dreams is to remain calm because overexcitement will wake you up.

Eye contact is important in lucid dreams involving sex as it is the brain's way of communicating consent to having a sexual encounter. Locking eyes with a dream character can be arousing in itself, and you might find that things move along swiftly after that.

Keep in mind that this is a dream, so your dream character could shape-shift during the process or not be who you thought at all. You might intend for it to be your husband only to find a few minutes into the experience that it is actually your boss or a celebrity crush. Your sexual partner might not even be human at all but rather take the shape of an animal or imaginary creature. Don't let this put you off. Instead, continue with the dream as normal and simply enjoy the experience. Let go of the control and immerse yourself fully into the actions so that you can broaden your mind to new ideas.

Lucid dreams are a safe space to explore your deepest sexual desires, so don't limit your thoughts at all. Use this opportunity to experience an orgy or take the role of the opposite gender to experience sex from their perspective. You could even decide to be an observer and feel the ecstasy by seeing other characters exploring their fantasies. Remain flexible throughout the dream. Since this is a safe space, you can withdraw your consent at any time, especially if dream sex evokes previous sexual trauma in the real world. Only do what you are comfortable with and wake yourself up if you have had enough.

Chapter 8:

Lucid Dreaming Is a

Practice for Life

Lucid dreaming may seem like an enhancement to your sleeping time, but it has more purposes than pure entertainment. Lucid dreaming training and techniques improve your awareness during daily life, and your nightly activities can help you work through challenging circumstances. Use your lucid dreams to understand yourself, your emotions, and other events better so that you can have a more fulfilling life.

Creative Problem-Solving

Creative thinking is something that everyone can do, but it is still a challenge for most people. Sometimes, the problem facing you seems impossible, and you have tried to find a solution, but you are stuck. Lucid dreaming is a great tool in this case because it does not have the confines of waking life. You can use your dreamscape to solve complex problems through visualization, and you can reject poor solutions quickly in favor of better options.

Lucid dreaming is a creative activity in itself, but you can use your dream in other ways. You could confide in your subconscious character about the problem and ask your dream to show you the answer. Another option is rehearsing for a show or an athletics meet until you get your technique exactly right. You can use your lucid dream in any way you wish, so push all boundaries out of the way and focus on finding the best solution.

Healing Dreams

Use your lucid dreams to boost your inner self and obtain some form of healing from emotional, mental, and physical problems. Your dreams have great power, so you can use them for so many things, including improvements to your life.

Treating PTSD

PTSD, or post-traumatic stress disorder, is a major mental health disorder a person may experience after a traumatic event that threatened their life or the life of someone else. Some people struggle to continue with their lives after such events, and they may experience night terrors, insomnia, flashbacks, or fear. Many people living with PTSD will lie awake because they fear having a traumatic nightmare, but you can use lucid dreams to deal with this trauma and sleep better.

Set a lucid dream intention to deal with your trauma. You don't have to face the entire event; rather, choose an aspect of the event to approach in your dream and deal with it amicably. It could be to create a dream character of a person you lost and say goodbye to them a final time, or maybe you want to replay a scene and observe your actions to make improvements in the future.

If you have PTSD and don't want to face your trauma, then that is fine too. You could use lucid dreaming to create a positive dream scene and escape from your traumatic reality. Knowing you can control your dream allows you to fall asleep more easily, and you know that you can escape a nightmare by waking up at will. Use your lucid dreams as a therapeutic activity and increase your waking awareness while using the relaxation activities to reduce tension.

Overcome Nightmares

Nightmares are one thing that can make you shout for help while asleep. Your nightmares could be works of fiction or have some truth behind them. Welcoming nightmares into your sleep and becoming lucid while they are happening allows you to address the underlying issues. Your physical body is safe in your bed, so let your mind explore your nightmare to stop it in its tracks.

Once you become lucid in your nightmare, say, "I'm dreaming," and do a reality check. The dreamscape can be quite terrifying, but you need to pinpoint what scares you most and approach that aspect. If you are uncertain about what is happening, then demand the dream to freeze so that you can observe your surroundings and find the problem. Alternatively, ask your subconscious for clarity.

Be courageous and face the problem in your nightmare. A threatening dream character should be approached carefully but in a friendly manner so that you show you are not a threat. Ask the figure how you can improve their experience—maybe that monster has a thorn in its paw, and after removing it, you can use the monster to explore the landscape as friends. Be compassionate to any threatening aspect of your dream and ask for clarity about the problem so that you can address it. A constructive dialogue could reveal more about your personality, such as worrying about your finances. Use those lessons in your waking life. If the character remains aggressive, then it might be better to remove your participation and wake yourself up from the dream.

Overcome Your Fears

Facing up to fears and phobias is something that few people want to do. If you don't like something in real life (like spiders, water, caterpillars, or knives), then you might not consider making them part of your dream scene. However, your dream world is a safe space, and these things cannot hurt you in your dreams, so you could use lucid dreaming to overcome your fears.

Try to set a dream intention to see a single thing of what you are afraid of—for example, a lone bird, spider, or car. Know that you will see this thing in your lucid dream and prepare for it. You could arrive in your lucid dream and find the fearsome object immediately or have to demand it as a dream object. Once you are face-to-face with your fear, ask it what it wants or why it is scary to understand your phobia properly. If an activity scares you, such as riding a motorcycle, then practice it over and over during your dream so that you become confident. It could take many dreams to overcome your fear but facing this issue can make your waking life a lot easier.

Stop Anxiety

Anxiety usually accompanies fear since the anxiousness is a response to what could happen if you had to experience this problem. Some people's anxiety stems from stress or traumatic events and can restrict their daily activities. Use your lucid dream to deal with your anxiety by rehearsing or observing difficult events. For example, you might experience anxiety at the thought of flying to a holiday destination and refuse to get on an airplane. Set a goal to go flying in an airplane in your lucid dream. Visualize the entire scene of getting onto the plane and enduring the trip. You might even go as far as captaining the plane. An incident-free flight could give you the confidence to try a flight in real life. Use this strategy with any anxiety-ridden event, no matter how big or small, so that you can live your life with less worry.

Improve Self-Confidence

Self-confidence is a belief in your abilities and believing that you have worth. Many people experience low self-confidence or have a dent in their confidence when it comes to specific activities. You can use lucid dreaming to improve your self-confidence by practicing things that you do poorly in your dreams. For example, you might need to do a presentation to a potential investor but lack public-speaking skills. Use your lucid dream to replicate the presentation environment complete with investors and give your presentation. Another example might be that you are struggling in your relationship due to poor communication, so spend time talking to your partner in your lucid dream. Repeat this simulation until you feel confident with whatever could boost your confidence.

Gain Self-Control

Self-control refers to your ability to control your own impulses and say "no" to yourself. You could struggle with self-control issues like an eating disorder, addiction, or compulsively doing an activity. Once you enter a lucid dream, you can replicate yourself to your wishes and encourage healthier habits. Your increased awareness in the dream state allows you to maintain self-control and might help you identify the triggers or aspects that affect your personality. Take your learnings from the dream world into the waking world so that you can practice self-control in real life.

Understanding Your Dark Side

Every person has a side to them that they suppress and refuse to let surface. This part of you is called a shadow archetype, which is a type of mental model that every person has. A shadow archetype is a dark side to a person that they don't want to show to others. You probably ignore that part of you entirely or be entirely unaware that you even have a dark side. The issues in your shadow archetype influence your behavior even if you do not realize it. To address these problems, you have to do shadow work, which includes exploring your ego while lucid dreaming and taking these learnings into the waking world.

Everyone Has a Dark Side

Yes, everyone does have a dark side, even if they don't want to admit it. You might call it weaknesses, hidden demons, or not acknowledge it all, but you should! The first thing you need to realize is that your shadow archetype is subconscious, so you might not recognize it all.

The part of your personality that suppresses your shadow is your ego who wants to protect you from getting hurt by the truth. Your ego helps you to function on a daily basis from childhood—it builds up walls from an early age. It is a self-preservation tool that makes you feel good, boosts your confidence, and helps you love yourself. It is a major part of your personality and helps you to survive. Your ego automatically pushes any bad feelings away from the forefront.

Maintenance Is Necessary

Think of your persona as a house for a moment. A house requires frequent maintenance to remain in good condition. It requires cleaning, tidying, painting, decorating, and throwing away trash. The same goes for your personality and mind—you have to keep it in a good condition; otherwise, it breaks into pieces. Your ego could be full of bad habits, traumatic events, or hidden demons, which need to be addressed before they cause damage. You need to take a long hard look at yourself and clean up so that your shadow archetype doesn't take over your life unintentionally.

Let's look at a few examples where people's shadow self is affecting their life:

A child may have been bullied at school, which made them feel inferior. As a protection mechanism, their ego encourages them to believe in themself and believe they are better than others, resulting in a superiority complex. This makes the person cocky and overly defensive or loud as they want themselves heard. Now, as an adult, the person continues to be rude and may wonder why people don't like being around them, or they could struggle to have a proper relationship. These defense mechanisms stem from childhood experiences, but the bullies no longer pose a threat, so this part of the shadow self should be cleaned out to change behavior and become a better person. In turn, the person can work on self-love, boosting their confidence, and being more compassionate towards others.

Another example is a child who grew up spoiled and getting anything they want because their parents couldn't spend time with them. In this case, the person learned to associate love with money and material items while suppressing feelings of being unloved due to a lack of attention. Around friends, the child boasts about all her toys and other material things so that she has some feeling of love. Later in life, this person may struggle with relationships, be called self-centered, or find all romantic relationships fail. At some stage, they may realize their narcissism and realize they need to practice self-love while opening their heart to other people.

These examples of shadow work indicate the complex nature of self and the role of your ego. Most shadow problems stem from childhood and might be suppressed for so long that you do not even think them to be a problem. Using lucid dreaming can help you to explore your shadow archetype so that you can realize the real problems and address them in an attempt to improve yourself and become a better person for it.

Shadow Work Is Challenging

Shadow work is not easy and requires months of exploration for a person to deal with their issues; however, it is a rewarding experience and allows you to move on with your life. It is a painful experience—confronting your problems is the only way to make constructive changes to your personality. This process cannot be rushed and will leave you feeling emotional, but you have to keep your focus on the long game and what you will achieve.

To do shadow work, you should:

- Be willing to open up about uncomfortable truths
- Be willing to identify, explore, and accept your weaknesses

- Have the courage to face your demons and acknowledge their existence
- Have an intense desire for self-improvement

Shadow work is difficult and can be a scary concept, but lucid dreaming can allow you to explore these issues safely. Remember that lucid dreams are a safe space, and you control the narrative so you can face your shadow at your pace and wake up if necessary. Be prepared for tough conversations and feelings of discomfort and realize that these lucid dreams will not be enjoyable, but they are meaningful.

Using Lucid Dreams for Shadow Work

Shadow work can be done in many ways and frequently pops up during psychotherapy sessions. Lucid dreams are another way to do shadow work and can reveal many things. Ensure you are adept at lucid dreaming and know the foundation and techniques well so that you can concentrate entirely on your shadow self.

ee. Identify Your Shadow

Your shadow self can appear in your dreams, both lucid and non-lucid, at any time and in any form. Use your dream recall and journal to look for dream signs that could be your shadow self. Specifically, look for a dream sign that causes feelings of fear, repulsion, or anxiety. It could be anything, so keep an open mind.

Some people find their shadow self to be a dirty animal, a haggard person, a book, or any other dream object.

ff. Engage Your Shadow

You can interact with anything in your lucid dream, so you need to do this with your shadow if you want to sort out your demons. Start by setting an intention to see your dream sign that you believe to be your shadow self. You can use any technique to summon a dream character, visualize them in your dream, or see them if they appear naturally.

Once you find your shadow in your lucid dream, you will need to confront it. Remember to approach your shadow self with love instead of disdain, because this is still a part of you that requires recognition and affection. You can walk up to your shadow self and give it a hug, send over ideas of compassion and love, or verbalize your intention. For example, you could walk up to the dream object with a friendly demeanor and say, "I want to know you better. What do you need?" Listen intently to what your shadow dream object has to say or reveal to you and let it take the lead in your dream.

gg. Accept the Shadow

You accept your shadow self as soon as you are willing to engage with it in a dream. Explore your shadow self with care and visit it frequently to understand yourself better. You could find this an easy process, or you might need time to accept what is happening and take smaller steps at a time.

hh. Take Your Shadow to the Waking World

The previous steps occur while you are asleep, but it is only meaningful if you take these teachings to the waking world. Write down all your shadow self insights in your dream journal as you recall your dreams. Take detailed notes and consider how you can improve yourself. Mindfulness techniques and meditation are ideal ways to work through these issues and practice self-love.

Adding Value to Your Lucid Dreams

Lucid dreaming teaches you tons about yourself, life, and society as a whole. It gives you amazing insights and helps you to solve tons of problems. The value of lucid dreaming is immense, especially if you master the techniques properly and use them to understand life better. Here are a few tips to get the most out of your lucid dreaming experience and make it a valuable part of your life.

Mindfulness is essential to lucid dreaming as it increases awareness. Always practice mindfulness strategies and concentrate on staying in the moment, even if you have no intention of lucid dreaming in the near future. Mindfulness also helps you to think critically about your surroundings and alerts you to lucid dreams, so prioritize these activities.

Your senses are an amazing tool that allows you to experience waking life, but they can fool you too, which means they are illusory. Use your senses to propagate great illusions in your dreams and encourage immersive experiences. Some of the best lucid dreams are rich in sensory stimulation and provide a feeling of refreshment and heightened sensitivity in the real world.

Welcome nightmares to your sleep cycle and use your awareness to have a fully lucid dream. Do not change your dream scene immediately; rather, spend some time to understand what is happening and probe the dream for deeper meaning. Nightmares frequently reveal more about yourself than you could ever imagine, and dealing with dream contents can be a freeing experience when faced with the waking world.

Waking up in the real world with a body still in sleep paralysis can be a frightening experience but consider yourself lucky—you have the ability to easily slip into a lucid dream because your mind is active while your body sleeps. Do not fight sleep paralysis or become stressed; rather, set a dream intention and start visualizing the dreamscape. It will provide an escape from the physical limitations of sleep paralysis while engaging your mind in a fantasy world.

Lucid dreaming boosts your creativity in the dreamscape while affecting it in the waking world too. While you are awake, your right brain is responsible for creative ideas, but your left brain frequently quashes this creativity through logical thinking. All lucidity practices require input from both brain hemispheres, which improves neuron communication and lucidity. Once you start dreaming, your right brain can create at full power because your left brain acknowledges it is a dream with zero limitations. This creative thinking can help you solve challenging life problems and allow you to put it in place in the waking life, albeit in measured quantities that you tested in your dreams.

Your dreams are as much a part of your life as your waking hours. Use your dreams to improve yourself and have a meaningful impact on your life. Set intentions for anything you need to confront, whether it be a phobia or your dark side, and keep a positive mentality. Your dreams can be a proactive tool to deal with many things, teach you more about yourself, and make a profound difference in your quality of life.

Conclusion

By this time, you have probably tried some of the lucid dreaming techniques and strategies already. I urge you to persevere in your lucid dreaming attempts and to continue along this journey as your abilities improve. Use this book frequently to practice mindfulness, take the teachings to heart, and ensure you are fully aware of what lucid dreaming entails for maximum effect.

The key to any lucid dream is to expect that you will become conscious and to incubate dream intentions properly. Take time to visualize your intended dreams so that you have a better chance of finding them when you become lucid. Enter your dreams with bold confidence in your abilities and expect to see results. Continuously work on achieving more while dreaming and verbalize your intentions to help you succeed.

Remember that lucidity equates to significant awareness, which is something you need to practice in your daily life if you want to use it properly in your dreams. Becoming lucid awakens your consciousness, so always do reality checks and verbalize that you are dreaming. Do grounding exercises and remain an active participant if you want your dream to intensify. Constantly scan your surroundings for ways to enhance your awareness, especially if the scene starts to fade.

Lucid dreaming requires constant practice and attention at all times of the day and night. Incorporate awareness strategies, dream journaling, and incubation into your lifestyle by making it a habit. Ensure the rest of your life is conducive to lucid dreaming by getting sufficient sleep, reducing stress, and living healthily. In turn, your lucid dreams will last longer, be meaningful, and enhance creativity.

Lucid dreaming has a greater purpose than simply living out your fantasies or exploring something new. It adds value to your life and can reveal truths about yourself that you do not know about. Use your lucid dreams to explore your personality and consider doing shadow work to improve yourself. It might not always be easy, but it can be an unburdening experience that lets you move on with your life.

You now have everything you need to become a lucid dreamer, so try one of the many challenges or create your own dream ideas. Practice the techniques frequently and focus on making lucid dreaming a part of your life. Enjoy the benefits of greater awareness and insights from lucid dreaming and apply them to your waking hours. I wish you stunning lucid dreams filled with your wildest desires!

If you found this book enjoyable and informative, then please leave a review on Amazon.

References

Altered States. (n.d.). *The Benefits of Lucid Dreaming.* https://altered-states.net/barry/newsletter482/

Amino. (n.d.). *Reality Shifting vs Astral Projection vs Lucid Dreaming.* https://aminoapps.com/c/realityshifting/page/blog/reality-shifting-vs-astral-projection-vs-lucid-dreaming/pXXz_34NHQuvp63wg1dvLdLlDxXJabXzD2

Breus, M. (2019). *6 Steps to Help You Remember Your Dreams.* Psychology Today. https://www.psychologytoday.com/us/blog/sleep-newzzz/201907/6-steps-help-you-remember-your-dreams

Britannica. (n.d.). *Frederik Willem van Eeden.* https://www.britannica.com/biography/Frederik-Willem-van-Eeden

Carr, M. (2020). *How Lucid Dreamers Say They Control Their Dreams.* Psychology Today. https://www.psychologytoday.com/us/blog/dream-factory/202006/how-lucid-dreamers-say-they-control-their-dreams

Cherry, K. (2019). *The Role of a Schema in Psychology.* VeryWell Mind. https://www.verywellmind.com/what-is-a-schema-2795873

Dream Hacking. (n.d.). *Lucid Dreaming & Spirituality: Achieving Spiritual Growth Through Lucid Dreams.* http://dream-hacking.com/lucid-dreaming-spirituality/

Dreaming Lucid. (n.d.). *The Science of Lucid Dreaming.* Lucid Dreaming Experience. https://www.dreaminglucid.com/the-science-of-lucid-dreaming/

DreamsCloud. (2017). *Why Do We Believe Dreams Are So Real While We're Dreaming?* Huffpost. https://www.huffpost.com/entry/dreams-feel-real_b_5652045?guccounter=1

Ennora. (n.d.). *What is the Difference Between Lucid Dreaming and Astral Projection.* https://www.ennora.com/blog/difference-lucid-dreaming-astral-projection/

Feldman, D. B. (2018). *Do Dreams Really Mean Anything?* Psychology Today. https://www.psychologytoday.com/us/blog/supersurvivors/201801/do-dreams-really-mean-anything

Gackenbach, J. & Bosveld, J. (1989). *Control Your Dreams*. New York, NY: Harper & Row Publishers.

Gassmann, C. (n.d.). *Paul Tholey and the Lucid Dream*. Traumring. http://traumring.info/tholey2.html

Gateway to Lucid Dreaming. (n.d.). *Using Dream Incubation to Create Your Dreams*. https://www.gateway-to-lucid-dreaming.com/dream-incubation.html

Hurd, R. (2021). *History of Lucid Dreaming: Ancient India to the Enlightenment*. Dream Studies Portal. https://dreamstudies.org/history-of-lucid-dreaming-ancient-india-to-the-enlightenment/

Johnson, C. (n.d.). *Deep Lucid Dreaming*. Create. https://deepluciddreaming.com/create/

Johnson, C. (n.d.). *Hypnagogic Imagery: Gateway to Lucid Dreaming*. Deep Lucid Dreaming. https://deepluciddreaming.com/2015/05/hypnagogic-imagery-as-a-gateway-to-lucid-dreaming/

King, B. (n.d.). *Lucid Dreaming Tips and Techniques*. Building Beautiful Souls. https://www.buildingbeautifulsouls.com/dream-interpretation-meanings/lucid-dreaming-tips-techniques/

LaBerge, S. & Rheingold, H. (1990). *Exploring the World of Lucid Dreaming*.

LaMarca, K. (2015). *Lucid Dreaming Therapy for Nightmares*. Mindful Lucid Dreaming. https://www.mindfulluciddreaming.com/post/2018/01/23/lucid-dreaming-therapy-for-nightmares

Lucidity.com. (1999). *A Study of Dreams by Frederik van Eeden*. http://www.lucidity.com/vanEeden.html

Lucid Dream Society. (2021). *14 Lucid Dream Myths You Need to Know*. https://luciddreamsociety.com/lucid-dream-myths/

Lucid Dream Society. (2021). *How to Stay in a Lucid Dream for Longer: 15 Ways*. https://luciddreamsociety.com/longer-lucid-dreams/

Lucid Dreams. (2013). *Tibetan Yoga and Secret Doctrines*. http://www.lucid-dreams.com/dreams/tibetan_yoga_and_secret_doctrine.htm

McNamara, P. (2011). *Dream and Reality*. Psychology Today. https://www.psychologytoday.com/us/blog/dream-catcher/201106/dream-and-reality

Meditation Mojo. (n.d.). *61 Points Relaxation Practice*. https://meditationmojo.com/61-points-relaxation-practice/

Mindfulness Exercises. (n.d.). *Awareness of Each of the Five Senses*. https://mindfulnessexercises.com/awareness-of-the-five-senses/

Murugesu, J. (2017). *Why Do our Dreams Feel so Real?* NewStatesman. https://www.newstatesman.com/2017/09/why-do-our-dreams-feel-so-real

Nunez, K. (2020). *The Benefits of Progressive Muscle Relaxation and How to Do It*. Healthline. https://www.healthline.com/health/progressive-muscle-relaxation

Spencer, R. M. C. (2019). *The Science of Dreams*. Frontiers for Young Minds. https://kids.frontiersin.org/article/10.3389/frym.2019.00140

The Occult Blogger. (2009). *Lucid dreaming - Peoples Testimonies*. https://www.occultblogger.com/lucid-dreaming-peoples-testimonies/

Trafton, A. (2019). *How Expectation Influences Perception*. MIT News. https://news.mit.edu/2019/how-expectation-influences-perception-0715

Turner, R. (n.d.). *12 Amazing Benefits of Lucid Dreaming*. World of Lucid Dreaming. https://www.world-of-lucid-dreaming.com/12-amazing-benefits-of-lucid-dreaming.html

The World of Lucid Dreaming. (2008-2018). https://www.world-of-lucid-dreaming.com/

Wilde, S. (2012). *Lucid Dreams*. Stuart Wilde. http://www.stuartwilde.com/2012/09/lucid-dreams/

Zugor, S. (n.d.). *The Complete History of Lucid Dreaming Explained Step by Step*. How to Lucid. https://howtolucid.com/lucid-dreaming-history/